Totkv Mocvse
NEW FIRE

Earnest Gouge, circa 1915,
National Anthropological
Archives #1127A.

Totkv Mocvse
NEW FIRE

Earnest Gouge, circa 1915,
National Anthropological
Archives #1127A.

Totkv Mocvse
NEW FIRE

CREEK FOLKTALES
BY Earnest Gouge

Edited and Translated by JACK B. MARTIN, MARGARET McKANE MAULDIN, *and* JUANITA McGIRT

Foreword by CRAIG WOMACK

Also by Jack B. Martin and Margaret McKane Mauldin

*A Dictionary of Creek/Muskogee, with Notes on the Florida and Oklahoma Seminole
    Dialects of Creek* (Lincoln, Nebr., 2000)

Publication of this book is made possible in part by a grant from the University of
Oklahoma Press Native Language Fund and Marcia Haag and Loretta Fowler, editors of
Chahta Anumpa: A Grammar of the Choctaw Language.

Proceeds from the sale of this work will go to Felix Gouge on behalf of the Gouge family.

Library of Congress Cataloging-in-Publication Data

Gouge, Earnest, ca. 1865–1955.
    Totkv mocvse/New fire : Creek folktales / by Earnest Gouge ; translated by Jack B.
Martin, Margaret McKane Mauldin, and Juanita McGirt ; foreword by Craig Womack.
        p. cm.
    Includes bibliographical references.
    ISBN 0–8061–3588–3 (cloth)
    ISBN 0–8061–3629–4 (paper)
    1. Creek Indians—Folklore. 2. Tales—Southern States. 3. Legends—Southern
States. 4. Creek language—Texts. I. Title: New fire. II. Title.

E99.C9G65 2004
398.2'089'97385—dc22

                                                                    2003063423

1   2   3   4   5   6   7   8   9   10

Contents

Illustrations

Photographs of Creek country by Jack B. Martin

Foreword

by Craig Womack

The work of Muskogee (Creek) author Earnest Gouge is part of one of the richest written tribal literary histories in North America, that of the Muskogee (Creek) Nation. Simply put, Earnest Gouge is an author, not an ethnographic respondent, even though we know he was associated with John Swanton, the famous southeastern ethnographer who asked him to write a collection of Creek stories. Swanton, however, chose not to include Earnest Gouge's work in his well-known collection of Southern Indian stories, possibly due to his inability to translate it. To what degree Earnest Gouge understood himself as a Muskogee author is difficult to say from this side of history. It would be a grave error, however, to fail to understand him as a Creek author since we have before us proof of some such conception on his part: he took pen in hand and produced a book-length manuscript.

When Earnest Gouge wrote these stories in 1915, Muskogee authorship was already an established tradition though much of it was yet to be discovered. George Stiggins, writing from his pre-removal home in Alabama during the 1830s, had authored a book entitled *Creek Indian History*, which took up the subject of the Red Stick War of 1813–14 and became a major source in the next century for John Swanton's southeastern studies and for student of early U.S. history. In addition to a gritty, compelling account of the war that divided the Creek Nation, Stiggins committed to writing important Muskogean narrative patterns, such as his description of the origins of Creek towns, a theme other Creek authors have emphasized in their books. In terms of Native literature more generally, Stiggins's book is one of the earliest Indian-authored tribal histories, preceded only by Tuscarora writer David Cusick's 1827 work, *Sketches of the Ancient History of the Six Nations*. Stiggins's foundational text was not published until 1989, though Swanton and others had read the manuscript much earlier. Swanton uses the manuscript as a source for his own writings on the Southeast. Whether or not Earnest Gouge would have known of Stiggins is difficult to say, though this is a possibility through the Swanton connection and by means of the incredible networking that has always linked the confederacy, even to the Alabama groups where George Stiggins stayed behind after Indian Removal.

Another Muskogee author who crossed paths with John Swanton is G. W. Grayson. Grayson, like George Stiggins, wrote a war narrative, in this case chronicling Grayson's own experiences as a Confederate officer in a Creek infantry unit during the Civil War. Like Stiggins's earlier work, it is a valuable historical source, particularly for its refusal to romanticize warfare. Earnest Gouge almost certainly would have known of G. W. Grayson, if not his efforts at authorship. In 1911, just before Gouge started his own stories for Swanton, Grayson met the ethnographer and become a major informant for his collection of southeastern stories, many of which Gouge himself would soon tell similar versions of. Swanton, in fact, read Grayson's Civil War chronicle and other shorter pieces he had written about Creek history. Here we discover a fascinating literary conundrum: why does Swanton's collection of "southeastern tales" contain animal stories but no narratives about, for example, Creek officers fighting on behalf of the Confederacy with whom their government had signed treaties and achieved representation in the Confederate congress? Swanton, obviously, perceived talking animal stories as Creek "culture"; whereas, relationships between sovereign governments somehow did not fit into his notion of Creek storytelling.

This dilemma will continue to haunt us up to our present literary moment when Indian stories, it would seem, unmarked by sufficient beads and feathers, usually are simply overlooked by Indians and non-Indians alike as authentic Native literature. Indian literature has suffered the burden of much of Indian Studies, which has been defined by cultural rather than legal criteria. This is relevant to the Gouge stories because we might wonder, had Earnest Gouge not been asked by John Swanton to author the story collection, might the content have been vastly different? Might Earnest Gouge's book, for example, be as reflective of his Four Mothers Nation activism opposing the dissolution of the Muskogee Nation after Oklahoma statehood and advocacy on behalf of the Treaty of 1832 as it is of traditional stories? Might political resistance, in fact, be a significant genre well within the parameters of traditional story-telling? As difficult as it is to know how Gouge may have perceived these issues, it is important that we imagine them. The Grayson manu-script, like Stiggins's, was not published until many years later, after its completion, when David Baird edited it and it became part of the University of Oklahoma Press catalog in 1988. Whether or not Gouge somehow read it, we must note that it would have been possible for him to view himself as a Muskogee author given those like Grayson, a man Gouge almost certainly would have known of, who had preceded him.

Another Creek literary source, actually published within Gouge's lifetime in 1891, was S. Alice Callahan's novel *Wynema: A Child of the Forest*. Although also Creek—her father was a prominent Muskogee politician—Callahan's and Gouge's social backgrounds were about as different as they possibly could be, and Callahan's novel is marked prominently by a southern white perspective (and here I am distinguishing her work from a southern mixed-blood Creek perspective since her novel notably erases Creek Christian and Creek mixed-blood political viewpoints, instead priortizing white Methodists as the center of its focus). Callahan treats the grounds-based ceremonial culture that marked Earnest Gouge's religious and political affiliations with disdain in her book and fails to give an accurate account of the history of Creek Christianity. Given the Gouge family's longstanding participation at the traditional Creek grounds, as well as the Creek churches, one can only guess what Earnest Gouge might have thought if he ever happened upon this ode to white Methodists. In terms of the bigger picture, we might simply note that it is likely he was aware of the fact that Creeks had been authors.

A popular Indian Territory writer whose name Gouge certainly would have recognized is Creek author Alexander Posey, especially given Posey's personal acquaintance with the Snake faction resistance leader Chitto Harjo, an important Four Mothers activist with whom Posey was at odds politically but held in high esteem nonetheless for his courage in pitting his group against the powers of the federal government. Posey's Fus Fixico letters, written at the turn of the century just before statehood, were popular in Territory newspapers such as the *Indian Journal*, the most widely-circulated paper where Earnest Gouge lived. The Fus Fixico letters could have served as a model for Gouge, especially in their representations of Creek speech. One of the many literary features of Gouge's stories, for example, is the spoken dialogue, which adds tremendous integrity to the unfolding of his narratives. While, surely, representations of speech are part of the oral tradition as well, one might wonder how Gouge came up with his system of quoting speakers in writing. At some juncture he had to deal with translating a spoken tradition into a textual one. It is likely he drew upon models, whether it was the Creek bible and hymnals or Creek authors. Although the marks of orality are present throughout his text, the book is also marked by literary techniques in its handling of quotations, plot, dramatic pacing, character development, and exposition of story details.

A serious further consideration, of course, given Gouge's choice to write in the Muskogee language, is whether or not he could read English. There was a significant proportion of the tribe in the early part of the century that could not speak English at all, much less read it. Whether or not he actively read Creek writers, however, Gouge surely understood writing as a Muskogee prerogative, arguably even as a burgeoning Muskogean tradition.

Outside of the literary world, at the time Earnest Gouge penned his work in 1915, Creeks were living in the political, social, and economic chaos that characterized the U.S. government's illegal dissolution of their former nation and the allotment of their tribal land. Moty Tiger was principal chief, the last to be elected for many years, followed by a string of presidential appointments, including G. W. Grayson himself upon Tiger's death in 1917. From its heyday of running social services, Creek Nation schools and orphanages, a supreme court and judicial system, a bicameral legislature, and a policing unit called the light horsemen, the principal chief's office had become largely a mop-up affair dealing with the troublesome reality that Creeks, though declared officially non-existent by the United States, still had everyday concerns that someone had to deal with.

In contrast to the official Creek government at Okmulgee that folded at the time of Oklahoma statehood was the group of Creeks who imagined the continuance of Creek sovereignty against all odds. The amazing story that contextualizes every word of Earnest Gouge's narratives is that, in spite of what Angie Debo characterized as the "road to disappearance," traditional Creeks like Earnest Gouge did anything but disappear. Gouge's

Creek activism was characterized by his participation in Four Mothers Nations, a pan-tribal group comprised of southeastern ceremonialists opposed to Oklahoma statehood and its implications for Indians. Four Mothers activities around the time Gouge was penning his stories included, but was not limited to, their retainer of lawyers in Washington, D.C., to combat the loss of children and lands due to court-appointed guardianships, their protest of the loss of the Creek lands of Four Mothers and Snake members who refused to sign allotment certificates, their fight against Oklahoma residency arguing that, among other things, they did not have to pay property taxes, their rally against poisoned whiskey containing wood alcohol that was being sold to young Creeks who drank it and died, and mass protest mailings of Mothers members' tax notices to the Secretary of the Interior in lieu of their tax payments. These battles were waged on many official fronts all the way from confronting local Indian Agents to the Attorney General's office; they were a concerted, organized, traditionalist bureaucracy that kept a continuous presence in Washington, D.C. In Oklahoma they maintained an organizational office in Hanna, where Earnest Gouge lived. As much as anything else, this is the tradition that Earnest Gouge writes from, a tradition that continued to recognize the validity of Creek governing traditions and to electing Creeks to political offices, long after the official Creek government at Okmulgee had been shut down.

The Snake and Four Mothers position was that even if no one else on the face of the earth recognized Creek government, if, in fact, the only place Creek government was recognized was inside the imaginations of Creeks who refused the death of their dreams and the meaning of constitutional law in a civilized society, such an imagining was still of utmost importance to their future. Without this faith in the perseverance of the Creek people, Gouge never could have penned his stories in the first place. One of the songs at the ceremonial grounds translates, "Long after

I die, this dance will continue." *Totkv Mocvse/New Fire* does not mark the road to disappearance. Belief in Muskogee continuance is the perspective of every story in this collection. Why do the Earnest Gouge stories differ so markedly from Swanton's representations of the same narratives? A likelihood is that, unlike Swanton, Earnest Gouge had no intention of recording the dying gasps of a doomed culture.

Turning directly to the stories, a significant feature is the way in which many of them unfold as fully developed narratives compared to the story fragments collected by Swanton and his predecessor W. O. Tuggle, whose work Swanton reprinted in his own collection. Stories like "The Hunter and His Dogs," for example, move through complete narrative cycles in which human and non-human relationships are fully explored. Stories that remain puzzling in Swanton, such as his incredibly brief representations of the turtle's checkered shell, become clear in the Gouge collection as we learn of the importance of male and female sexuality, the realms of women's and men's knowledge, and the way in which these worlds both overlap and remain separate. Multiple story versions, such as the story of turtle being beaten by three mothers, as well as the turtle looking up the women's dresses, give us a clear indication of turtle's tendency to lewd comments and actions, which helps explain why someone might be tempted to beat him with a sofkey pestle. (Creek elder Linda Alexander has also contributed to our understanding of the turtle story by telling fuller versions and interpreting them and elaborating the male-female relations that are strong parts of the story. Interestingly, her renditions corroborate Gouge's versions.)

The stories reveal unique features of a Creek sense of narrative history in the use of dialogue tags such as "They are doing exactly what I said, she said, it was said" (17), which marks the Creek propensity for drawing attention to the layered effect of narrative by highlighting the interaction between the storyteller who quotes characters, the characters' own rela-

tionships to others in the story, and the community of people who comment on and pass down these tellings. Such dialogical grounding devices create a conversation with the text and its readers and remind us that the story is not simply about a dog and hunters but our own place within various communities with which we share responsibilities, including the responsibility of knowing something about history, about those things of which "it was said," and the act of saying them.

These stories go beyond the usual Indian clichés. Rabbit, we find out, not only has visited overseas but learns that there are Creek towns there that stomp dance! He also gets instruction from God, who tells him, essentially, that he is already too damn smart for his own good. These are not the least-Indian stories, the suspect Indian stories, the ones earlier ethnographers like Swanton tried to disclaim for their European underpinnings. These are Creek through and through, refreshingly original, authentic because of their capacity to take in new realities, to function as a living tradition.

Given the wonderful inclusion of the Creek language originals in this book, these stories are destined to become an important part of Creek language instruction in Oklahoma, Alabama, Georgia, Florida, and elsewhere. The collection is one of the great finds in Creek literary history. Margaret Mauldin, also known as Mvhayv, and her daughter Gloria McCarty, also known as Mvhayuce, have been instrumental in founding a Creek pedagogy on the University of Oklahoma campus. Imagine developing a curriculum in a language for which no instructional texts existed. This is the situation they found themselves in when they came to the University of Oklahoma to teach Creek, and they have done a remarkable job of developing a system for understanding Muskogee. Their continuing devotion to illuminating the uncertainties of the language is truly inspiring. Jack Martin, a southeastern specialist and linguist who worked with Margaret and Gloria on a new Creek dictionary, has been an important collaborator in that work as well as on the Earnest Gouge stories. Juanita McGirt, Margaret Mauldin's sister, is co-translator of the collection at hand and is a respected Creek elder.

Creek authorship continues at a phenomenal rate and includes tribal histories, autobiographies, novels, short stories, works of poetry, plays, traditional stories, accounts of Vietnam veterans' experiences, late-nine-teenth-century arguments for women's suffrage, explorations of Muskogee philosophy, life stories of medicine people, and much more. Truly, it is a new fire, which life at the grounds teaches us is dependent on all the fires that came before.

Acknowledgments

Totkv mocvse (new fire) is a term used for the ceremonial fire marking the rebirth of a tribal town. We hope this work will rekindle interest and pride in the Creek language and in Earnest Gouge and other keepers of Creek traditions.

We are grateful to the Smithsonian Institution's National Anthropological Archives for allowing us to publish these texts and for making photographs and photocopies of the originals available to us.

Felix Gouge provided enthusiastic support for the project, shared his family history, and showed us his grandfather's home, church, and ceremonial ground. Edna Gouge introduced us to other family members and provided encouragement.

Alice Snow, Happy Jones, and Ralph Heneha, Jr., told us their versions of stories and helped with older words.

Gloria and Michael McCarty made sound recordings of Margaret Mauldin reading the stories. Jesse Mercer and Virginia Crowell helped with the typing. Pamela Innes, Jason Jackson, and Craig Womack provided helpful comments.

The National Endowment for the Humanities (Grant RT-2156694) and the National Science Foundation (Grant SBR-9809819) funded this research as part of a larger project to document the Creek language.

To all who have helped, we say, *Mvto!*

*Earnest Gouge in later life,
courtesy of Felix Gouge.*

Introduction

by Jack B. Martin

The stories in this collection were written by Earnest Gouge for John Reed Swanton in 1915. They were written in Creek (Muskogee) and are translated here into English for the first time.

Earnest Gouge's life spanned a period of dramatic change. For centuries, the Creeks had lived on the Coosa, Tallapoosa, Alabama, Chattahoochee, and Flint rivers of Alabama and Georgia. From 1836 to 1837, the United States forced the majority of Creeks to take up new lands in the east-central portion of Indian Territory, where they formed (and still maintain) a democratic government with a constitution, a legislature, schools, laws, and courts. Many families raised crops and livestock. Individuals belonged to the Creek Nation, but also to an older form of government based on the tribal town (*etvlwv*). Each tribal town sent representatives to the Creek Nation and hosted a Green Corn celebration in the summer. Some individuals also belonged to a church, where songs and sermons were in Creek. Newspapers, readers, songbooks, a dictionary, laws, and other publications exposed individuals to the written form of the language.

Earnest Gouge was born around 1865. He may have learned to read Creek and English in school or through the church. When he was in his twenties and thirties, the United States again began to attack the foundations of Creek society. In 1898, the United States dismantled the Creek court system and forced the Creek Nation to convert its lands to privately owned tracts. Oklahoma became a state in 1907, when Gouge was in his forties. For the rest of his life, Creeks would fight to regain their sovereignty.

As a result of these events, Gouge became a political activist, traveling to Washington and criticizing the United States for failing to abide by its treaties. Gouge appears to have met John Reed Swanton (1873–1958) around 1915, eight years after Oklahoma statehood. Swanton was an ethnographer and a historian at the Bureau of American Ethnology who was to become a major figure in southeastern studies. One of his ambitions was to gather myths and tales from southeastern tribes in the original languages, to have these translated, and to study the language and beliefs of the group through the resulting materials. If his sources were literate, he arranged to have them write down stories.

F. W. Hodge (1923: 10) clarifies Swanton's arrangements for acquiring texts:

> From the end of September until the latter part of November, 1915, Dr. Swanton was in Oklahoma, where he collected 113 pages of Natchez text from one of the three surviving speakers of the language; he also spent about three weeks among the Creek Indians, where about 80 pages of myths in English were procured. Further ethnological material was also obtained from the Creeks and from the Chickasaw, to whom a preliminary visit was made. While with the former people Dr. Swanton perfected arrangements with a young man to furnish texts in the native language, which he is able to write fluently, and in this way 173 pages have been submitted, not including translation.

The "young man" in question was Earnest Gouge, then about fifty years old. The 173 pages he transcribed were written in a version of the traditional

Creek spelling system developed in the nineteenth century. The original manuscript is now housed at the Smithsonian Institution's National Anthropological Archives in Suitland, Maryland, where it is catalogued as follows:

> Gouge, Earnest. Creek texts, with English titles and occasional English translations by John R. Swanton. 1906–1930. Manuscript 4930, Smithsonian Institution National Anthropological Archives.

Swanton acquired translations of a few of the stories and had the manuscript typed, but never finished editing it.

I ran across the Gouge manuscript in 1994. I sent a photocopy to Margaret Mauldin, a close friend and Creek instructor at the University of Oklahoma. She praised them, noting that they often contained fuller versions of stories now heard in fragmented form. She introduced me to her friend Edna Gouge, Earnest Gouge's grandniece. Edna explained the Gouge family history and introduced us to Earnest Gouge's grandson Felix, a respected member of New Tulsa tribal town.

With Felix Gouge's permission, we then set about translating and editing the manuscript. Margaret's daughter Gloria McCarty and son-in-law Michael owned a recording studio, so one of our first steps was to make sound recordings of Margaret reading the originals. Margaret then retranscribed the originals into a more standard version of the Creek alphabet, and her sister Juanita McGirt added English translations. Two students helped type the materials, I secured funding and began editing them, and Margaret corrected the translations. I also worked on diplomatic versions of the stories (facsimiles reflecting Gouge's own spelling) and phonemic versions (accurate records of vowel length, accent, etc.), based on Margaret's sound recordings, the originals, and interviews. Meanwhile, Felix Gouge explained more about the Gouge family history and showed us his grandfather's house, ceremonial ground, church, and burial site.

We decided to distribute the materials connected with this project through different media. In 2002, the Creek Nation had a population of fifty-two thousand. We felt this audience would be best served by parallel Creek-English versions of the stories and sound recordings on an accompanying disk. The recordings were included to preserve the sound of Creek and to make the stories accessible to Creek speakers who do not read. More technical materials (diplomatic and phonemic versions of the stories) have been published at www.wm.edu/linguistics/creek. Copies of these same materials will be archived at the National Anthropological Archives.

About Earnest Gouge

Earnest Gouge and his younger brother Jack (more commonly known as *Cake Rakko* or Big Jack) were full-blood Muskogees born in Indian Territory around the close of the U.S. Civil War, a time when battles within the Five Tribes echoed the larger conflict in the United States. According to Felix Gouge, Earnest and Jack were abandoned or orphaned as children and taken to Arbeka tribal town in the Creek Nation, Indian Territory (J. Martin 1997). Thomas Red, a preacher at Hillabee Baptist Church, adopted the boys and raised them as his own.* Though the boys were raised in the church, they began going to ceremonial grounds as soon as they were old enough.

Earnest and Jack married two sisters named Nicey and Lucinda who were residents of Hanna and members of Hillabee Canadian tribal town.

* Confirming the family history, the Creek Nation rolls approved in 1902 list Earnest and Jack Gouge as nephews of Thomas Red (Dawes Roll numbers 8496–98). Their father is listed as Dave George of Tuckabatchee, with mother unknown. We follow these rolls and the Smithsonian in using the spelling "Earnest" instead of "Ernest."

Earnest and Nicey had four sons spaced two years apart: Pewter (better known as *Kv-Rakko* or Big Head), Sam (*Same*), Fred (*Sakco* or Crawdad), and Albert (*Vlpvtv* or Alligator). According to family history, Earnest and Jack were nephews of the famous Opothleyahola ("Old Gouge"), chief of the Upper Creeks from 1828 to 1863 and leader of the northern faction of Creeks during the Civil War.*

Earnest and Jack were interested in seeing that the United States lived up to the treaties signed by their uncle. This interest led them to become involved in a group known as the Four Mothers (*Ecke Ostat*), an early intertribal organization of Creeks, Cherokees, Choctaws, and Chickasaws that continued into the 1940s.

Collections raised by the Four Mothers enabled Earnest, Jack, and an interpreter to travel to Washington, D.C. The Creek representatives were given medallions, while the Cherokee representatives were given beaded belts. The medallions and belts had images of clasped hands on them and were thought to serve as keys to the capital.

In 1915 Earnest Gouge was living on his allotment near Hanna, with a small house and barn close to his church (Hillabee Baptist) and tribal town (Hillabee Canadian). Felix Gouge remembers that his grandfather would tell stories while driving or after dinner. In the winters he would fill his stone fireplace with green wood to last the night and sit with his back to the heat while others gathered before him. As an older man he turned to preaching, though he continued to take medicine at his ceremonial ground. A favorite activity was fish-kills, in which fish were drugged and shot with arrows.

Jack Gouge (Cake Rakko or Big Jack) holding medallions, courtesy of Felix Gouge.

* Meserve (1931) and Carter (1979) provide accounts of Opothleyahola's life. Several Creek freedmen interviewed in the Federal Writers' Project in the 1930s refer to Opothleyahola as "Old Gouge." Lucinda Davis (Baker and Baker 1996:109) was recorded as saying, "My mammy was Serena and she belong to some of de Gouge family. Dey was big people in de Upper Creek, and one de biggest men of the Gouge was name Hopoethleyoholo for his Creek name. He was a big man and went to de North in de War and died up in Kansas, I think."

Earnest Gouge died at about the age of ninety, after his younger brother Jack. He was hit by a car while riding a horse, finally succumbing to his injuries on September 4, 1955. To the best of our knowledge, these are the only writings he left, though he also dictated three Creek texts about ball games and his tribal town for Mary R. Haas (Haas 1939). He is buried facing his ceremonial ground.

About the Stories

The stories in the Gouge manuscript cover a wide range of themes. Many are of the Uncle Remus type, involving the humorous adventures of Rabbit, Wolf, and other animals with human characteristics. Others are hunting stories designed to scare a nighttime audience. Some refer to a time when bows and arrows were used; others refer to guns and shot pouches. In every case, the stories are meant to be shared among adults for amusement and are thus folktales. Stories of this type (called *nak-onvkuce* in Creek) were told at any time of year, around the fire or after a meal, and are typical of stories commonly traded before the advent of television.

Many of the stories (e.g., "The Young Man Who Turned into a Snake") are told by tribes elsewhere in the Southeast and beyond and may be ancient. For these, comparisons with neighboring groups (e.g., Mooney 1900; Wagner 1931; H. Martin 1977; Lankford 1987; Jumper 1994; Grantham 2002) and standard comparative folklore indices and classifications (Thompson 1955–58, Aarne and Thompson 1964) are useful. Some (e.g., "Rabbit Seeks Wisdom from God") may be African in origin (Dundes 1969; Bascom 1992). A few (e.g., "The Three Brothers and the Spotted Horse") are not well known even among Creek speakers and may have been personal favorites of Gouge's.

Occasionally an attempt is made in a story to explain some aspect of the natural world (why Opossum's tail is bare, why Turtle's shell is cracked, why bodies of water have particular shapes). As Howard N. Martin (1977:xxv) has observed, explanations of this kind are designed to convince the listener of a story's truth and are not the focus of a story.

The number four, associated with the four cardinal directions and with the four medicine colors (red, white, black, yellow), figures prominently in Creek stories. Important actions are done four times to signal completeness: when Turtle races Wolf, they thus decide the course will cover four ravines.

Several of the stories in this collection are similar, though not identical, to stories in Tuggle (1973) and Swanton (1929). Indeed, one of the sources Swanton names for his stories is "Big Jack of Hilibi," Earnest Gouge's younger brother. It may be that Jack was enlisted to tell the stories in English, while his older brother was persuaded to write them in Creek. The exact versions in the present collection appear not to have been used by Swanton, however, since he lacked English translations for most of them.

For convenience, a summary is presented immediately preceding each story, with cross-references to Swanton's 1929 collection. A few comments about each story have also been added. A number of other published sources may be consulted for further information on Creek history and culture (see, among others, Speck 1907; Swanton 1922, 1928; Debo 1941; Lewis and Jordan 2002).

Transcription and Translation

Creek is an endangered language. In editing this manuscript, we wanted first to make the materials available to the Gouge family and to the larger Creek community. Gouge made little use of punctuation, and the spelling he used was a simplified version of the spelling used in the Creek first and second readers (Robertson and Winslett 1867, 1871). In order to make the manuscript more accessible, we added punctuation (uppercase letters, commas, periods, divisions into paragraphs) and titles, and converted Gouge's spelling to a more standard version that students might use. Where his spelling reflected an older pronunciation, we tried to preserve it. Thus, Gouge, like many of his contemporaries, said *echustake* 'egg' where many speakers today say *eccustake*.

The accompanying sound recordings sometimes differ in small ways from the written version presented here. The recordings were made early in the project, with Margaret Mauldin reading from photocopies of the original manuscript. Later study sometimes led us to revise our interpretation of specific words, so that small differences are sometimes apparent between the various versions.

The order of stories presented here is the same as in the original manuscript, though one story fragment has been omitted. The story "Girl abducted by Lion" appears twice in the original collection: the first time, it is placed after "Rabbit steals fire," but is missing the first page. The second time, it appears intact as the final story, with slightly different wording. We assume that the first page was lost at an early date and that Swanton asked Gouge to rewrite the story. We have included only the complete version in this collection, placed at the end.

As might be expected, many of the words in the stories raise issues in translation. A case in point is the character *Este-Papv*. This term is literally 'person-eater' and is taken by modern Creek speakers to refer to a lion. Even though lions are not native to the Americas, the term has been used in Creek to mean 'lion' since at least 1860 (Buckner and Herrod 1860:44). Swanton (1929:20) translated it as Lion or Man-Eater, but Mary R. Haas, based on later fieldwork, defined it as "a cannibalistic character appearing in myths" (Haas ca. 1940). It seems clear from the plots of the stories (e.g., "Rabbit traps Lion on the other side of the ocean") that Gouge had the lion in mind rather than a cannibal or a panther. Knowledge of lions (and stories about them) might have passed between Africans and Creeks.

In editing and translating the stories, we struggled with the many grammatical and stylistic differences separating Creek and English. The Creek sentences in these stories are often quite long, consisting of chains of loosely linked clauses. At times we felt it necessary to divide these long chains into smaller units by adding three dots (...) at natural breaks. When a sentence does end in Creek, the topic is often resumed by use of a reduced clause (*momen* 'be so, and', *monkv* 'so', *mohmen* 'then', *momis* 'but', etc.) at the beginning of a new chain. We considered highlighting this structural aspect of Creek by using a verse translation of the stories in which each of these connecting words might be given a fixed translation, as in the following passage from the first story:

<u>*Momen*</u> *mvn okakekv, vtutketv hopokv vpēyvtēs.*
<u>*Momet*</u> *fullof, este hvmket vnrapvtēs.*
<u>*Momen*</u> *'tem punahoyen...*

<u>And</u> meaning what they said, they went in search of work.
<u>And</u> while they were about, a man met them.
<u>And</u> they spoke with him...

Creek speakers we have asked tend to dislike these translations: a common reaction is that "there are too many *momen*'s" in the stories. Verse translations place too much attention on normal sentence structure and lead to the erroneous view that connecting words have fixed equivalents in English.

A second difficulty is the very different styles of reporting speech in Creek and English. As the rather literal English translation below shows, Creek tends to frame a quotation with verbs meaning 'say' or 'tell' before and after the quotation:

Momet okakat,
  Vtutketvn hopoyet fulletvn puyacet os,
kicet, erken em pohaken

And saying,

    We want to go around looking for work,

  they said, and asked their father

To make the English more natural, we have omitted some of these verbs in the translation. A further difficulty is that Creek makes extensive use of direct quotation (*"We want to go around looking for work," they said*), while it is often more natural in English to use indirect quotation (*They said they wanted to go around looking for work*). In this case we have sometimes stretched the English by using direct quotation, but English is often hard to follow when quotations occur within quotations:

Cecke nakvlke toyēs, makētvnka? kicaken...

Konovlke toyēs, makētvnks, kicaken...

Did your mother say what clan we are?

She used to say we're Skunk clan, they said...

The second line here is literally "'"We are Skunk clan," she used to say,' they said...." In this case, we have used indirect quotation in the English to make it more readable, and have omitted quotation marks because of their complex layering.

Our English translations also attempt to preserve Creek phrases like *mahokvnts* 'it was said' or *onahoyvnts* 'it was told', phrases used at the beginnings and ends of stories to acknowledge other sources and to invoke a line of storytellers stretching from the present to a mythic past.

Two types of songs (*yvhiketv*) appear in Creek stories. One type is a medicine chant (*heleshakv yvhiketv*), illustrated here by the one Turtle uses to mend his shell in stories 7 and 27. A similar type of chant is used in story 28 when Fawn uses a wolf's bones to put a hex on wolves, and in story 29 when Lion uses a stone disk to divine a path. A different type of song is evident in story 13, when Lion sings forlornly of having eaten the people in the southwest, and in story 29, when the girl laments not being with her brothers. This latter type was typically sung with a melody rather than chanted, though the tune is not preserved in this manuscript.

The Creek Alphabet

The Creek spelling used here evolved during the mid-nineteenth century and is discussed more fully in Martin and Mauldin (2000). The most common phonemic equivalent of each letter is presented below in slashes (/ /):

a   /a:/   *afke* /á:fki/ 'hominy grits'. As in English *father*.

c   /c/   *cesse* /císsi/ 'mouse'. As in English *inch*.

e   /i/   *ecke* /ícki/ 'his/her mother'. As in English *if*.

ē   /i:/   *ēcko* /í:cko/ 'dried corn'. As in *feed*.

f   /f/   *fo* /fó:/ 'bee'. As in English *foot*.

h   /h/   *hvse* /hasí/ 'sun'. As in English *head*. When doubled, it has a rougher quality approaching *kh*.

i   /ey/   *ehiwv* /ihéywa/ 'his wife'. As in English *hey*.

k   /k/   *kapv* /ká:pa/ 'coat'. As in English *skirt*.

l   /l/   *lucv* /locá/ 'turtle'. As in English *light*.

m   /m/   <u>m</u>ēkko /mí:kko/ 'chief'. As in English <u>m</u>ouse.

n   /n/   <u>n</u>erē /niłí:/ 'night'. As in English <u>n</u>ight.

o   /o:/   <u>o</u>fv /ó:fa/ 'inside'. As in English r<u>o</u>de.

p   /p/   <u>p</u>enwv /pínwa/ 'turkey'. As in English s<u>p</u>in.

r   /ɬ/   <u>r</u>vro /ɬaɬó/ 'fish'. A little like *thl* in English *fif<u>thl</u>y*, except that the air passes over the sides of the tongue rather than the tongue tip.

s   /s/   <u>s</u>ukhv /sókha/ 'hog'. Approximately as in English <u>s</u>un.

t   /t/   <u>t</u>afv /tá:fa/ 'feather'. As in English s<u>t</u>iff.

u   /o/   f<u>u</u>swv /fóswa/ 'bird'. As in English p<u>u</u>t.

v   /a/   <u>v</u>ce /ací/ 'corn'. As in English <u>a</u>go.

w   /w/   <u>w</u>otko /wó:tko/ 'raccoon'. As in English <u>w</u>in.

y   /y/   <u>y</u>vnvsv /yanása/ 'buffalo'. As in English <u>y</u>ellow.

vo   /aw/   h<u>vo</u> /hâw/ 'okay'. As in English l<u>ow</u>.

ue   /oy/   hop<u>ue</u>take /hopoy-tá:ki/ 'children'. As in English b<u>oy</u> or sometimes as in qu<u>ee</u>n.

When vowels and diphthongs are nasal, they are written with a hook underneath: ą /a:ⁿ/, ę̄ /i:ⁿ/, etc. Brackets ([   ]) appear around elements that were omitted in the Creek or that help clarify the English translation. Words for animals (*Cufe* 'Rabbit', *Yvhv* 'Wolf', etc.) are capitalized when they are felt by native speakers to be names. Lowercase is used when they are preceded by a demonstrative (*mv cufe* 'that rabbit').

The main difference between Gouge's spelling and that used here is in the vowels. In most cases, Gouge wrote *a* for both *a* and *v*, and *e* for both *e* and *ē*. He generally used *u* or *oe* for the diphthong *ue*, and *aw* for the diphthong *vo*. The page from the manuscript shows some of the differences between Gouge's spelling and our own. A typescript of Gouge's original spelling is available at www.wm.edu/linguistics/creek.

First page of the Gouge manuscript. "Creek" and "Three Brothers" are in
John Swanton's hand. Smithsonian Institution, National Anthropological
Archives: Ms. 4930.

The Stories

1

The three brothers and the spotted horse

Three brothers are hired to catch something stealing crops. The younger brother succeeds and catches a magical horse, who gives him a whistle. The older brothers torment the boy, but the boy is able, with the help of the horse, to marry a beautiful woman and gain wealth. The older brothers tell their father that the youngest brother is dead, but he eventually rejoins his father and the older brothers are chased off.

This story is not well known. The father and the youngest son are both trusting. The youngest son never tries to get revenge and is richly rewarded.

Este-vcule hvmket eppucetake tuccēnen ocēt likvtēs. Momen mv cēpvnvke tuccēnat vkerrickv hayakvtēs. Momet okakat, Vtutketvn hopoyet fulletvn puyacet os, kicet, erken em pohaken, erke tat mvo 'moh-vkvsamvtēs. Momen mvn okakekv, vtutketv hopokv vpēyvtēs. Momet fullof, este hvmket vnrapvtēs. Momen 'tem punahoyen, ayen momusen vtutketv hopoyvlket fullet omen kērrof, mv este vnrapē huerat vtutketv ocēt omvtet em onayvtēs. Momet okat, Naket tạyen vnnokset ont os. Momat nerē min omēpet ont omen... Mvn estit mv nake noksē arat wicēcesasen omat, cvtoknawv cukpe-hvmken, pale-cahkēpen ($150.00) cenfēkarēs. Monkv mvn vtutketv ocis, kicet em onayet respoyof, Pont omeyvrēs, makakvtēs.

Momen mv este arat encukon fekhonnet vpokvtēs. Momen mv vtutketv epucaset omaket onkv, momusen mv 'svculvkuecat mit enhomvn nake epokv tat komet welakvtēs.

Momen mv 'svculicat hvmket ayvtēs. Yomocket omen, ayet omvtēs. Momēt aret erohhvyatket rvlaken, cvpofv-pucaset em pohet, Naket noksekon hvyatkehaks? kicet em pohen... Naket noksekon hvyatket os, kicen... Mon omat ahyit erhēcin momēpet on oketsken omat, cenfēkarēs, kihcet ayvtēs (cvpofv-pucase hecvranet). Mont aret eroran, cvpofv nake noksē arvtē hvtvm noksepēt oman ohkvten hehcet, eratet rvlahket okat, Naket noksekon hvyatkes mahketskat, noksepēt oman oketsket onkv, cenfēkvko tayet os, kihcen... Hvtvm hvmket okat, Vnet omarēs, naket aret nokset on omat, maket omen... Mon omat, yomockat ahyet, naket aret nokset on omat, fekhonnicvs! kihcet, cvpofv-pucaset vtotvtēs.

An old man lived with his three sons. Now the three boys made some plans. We want to go around looking for work, they said, and asked their father, and their father, too, agreed. And meaning what they said, they went in search of work. While they were going about, a man met them. So they spoke with him, and as soon as he learned that they were job hunters, the man who had met them said that he had work. Something's devouring my crops, he said.* It happens at night... If anyone can stop that greedy thing, I'll pay you one hundred and fifty dollars ($150.00). So I have that job, he said, and when he finished telling them [that], they said, We'll do it.

So it was that they stayed awhile at the man's house. And having accepted the job, right away the older two wanted the pay first.

Now the oldest one went. It was getting dark, so he started out. He went and returned the next morning, and the owner of the field asked him: Had nothing devoured my crops by dawn? Nothing had devoured your crops by dawn, he said... Well, then, I'll go and see, and if it's as you say, I'll pay you, he said, and left (the owner of the field was going to see). And when he got there, he saw that, despite the report, something had been in his field again, devouring his crops, and coming back, he arrived, saying, You said nothing had devoured my crops by dawn, but because it has, I cannot pay you... Once more another one said, I'll do it, if there is some-thing going around devouring crops, he said... Well, then, go, and when it gets dark, whatever's out there devouring crops, stop him! the owner of the field said to him and sent him off.

* The verb *noksetv*, used throughout this story, implies greed ('to hog'), often associated with food ('to make a pig of oneself on', 'to feast oneself on') without implying that all the food or crops have been consumed.

Mohmen mvn okekv ayvtēs, nake noksv sumecicvranat. Momet mi cvpofvn erohhvyatket rem paksen rvlakvtēs.

Momen cvpofv-pucaset em pohet okat: Mucv tv? Naket noksekon hvyatka? kicen... Mucv tat naket noksesekon hvyatkes, kicet em onayvtēs. Momen okat, Mon omat, ahyit erhecin... Naket noksepekot on omat, cenfēkarēs, kihcet ayvtēs.

Mont aret mv cvpofv ahyet eroran, mv nake noksē arvtē hvtvm noksehpet sumkēpet oman okēpen... Erhēcet ervlahket okatet, Naket noksepekot os, maketsket ont omis, momat noksepēt omēpan oketsket onkv, fēkvko tayētt os, kicvtēs.

Momen mv cēpvnvke eryopv arat okatet, Vntat fekhonnicvyēs—naket aret omen omēto 'stomis, maket omen... Mv ervhvlket okakat, Mv mahvkvts. Naken estonhkos, kicaket ehvnaket oman, mv cēpvnē yopv arat vwicēcekatēs. Momen cvpofv-pucaset okatet, Mon omat, celayet hēcetskēs, kicvtēs.

Momen mv cēpanat mv cvpofv vyvranē em etetakat, mv cvpofv-pucasen empohet okat, 'kvhakucen cokv eshvmken esvmes, kicen, esēmvtēs.

Momen hvtvm, Eswvnakucen hvtvm vmes, kicen, mvo ēmvtēs. Mohmen vyēpvtēs. Yomuckeko monken, ayvtēs.

Mont erohret, estvn acēyet omvtē em vketēcet aret, esenhēcvtēs. Mohmet mv acēyvtē mạhusan mv eswvnakuce enpoloksihcet em vtarvtēs. Mohmet ervtēpet totkv etecēpet taklikvtēs. Momet nockvn ēlen omat,

Then saying that, [the second son] went to get rid of the crop-eating thing. And he spent the night in that field and returned the next day.

Then the owner of the field questioned him: What about this time? Did nothing devour my crops by dawn? he asked him. This time nothing devoured your crops by dawn, he told him. Then [the owner] said, Well, then, I'll go and see... If nothing has eaten my crops, I'll pay you, he said, and started off.

Going there, he got to the field, and contrary to the report, the thing going around devouring crops had again devoured his crops and vanished... Coming back from checking, he said, You said nothing had devoured my crops, but because it did devour my crops, I cannot pay.

Then the youngest of the boys said, I can stop it—whatever it is going around, he said... His brothers said, He can't do anything, and scolded him, but the youngest boy wouldn't quit. Then the owner of the field said to him, Well, then, you can try handling it.

And as the boy was preparing to go to the field, he asked the owner of the field, saying, Give me a package of straight pins, and he gave them to [the boy].

And again he said, Give me some rope, and that, too, he gave him. Then he started off. Before it got dark, he left.

He got there, checked around, and found where [the thing eating the crops] had been getting in. Then right where he had been coming in, he made a loop with the rope and hung it for him. Then he came back, lit a 'kvhakucen vccetvn vcakcvhēt hvmkvn hahyet, mvn esnvtaksēn espvticet nocen omat, mvn ohlatket ohpvlpaket ēyvhonecicet taklikēpvtēs.

Momen ayen yomuckvtē hofunē haken 'stvrakecicvcoken pohat, Cewvnahyvkvyvc[oks] cē! mahket, ayet eroran, cerakko cvlahusēt ohmvtet hueren erorvtēs.

Momen mvn eroran vtēkusen, mv cerakko-cvlahet okat, Vnrecvpvs. 'Svnvcomvn nokisvkos, kicen... Okatet, Cenrecvpvko tayētt os, cvpofv-pucaset ceheceko vtēkat, kicet omen... Okat, Nvcǫmen cenfēhokvranen omehaks? kicet em pohen... Cukpe-hvmken pale-cahkēpen ($150.00) vnfēhokvranet omet os, kicen... Mon omat, vneu matvpomen cenfēkarēs. Mohmet estvn estomēn aret ometske estomis, kohv-motken cēmin... Mvn ocēt aret vcvkerricetsken omen omat, ecepakit, naket estomēpēto 'stomis, ecepakarēs, kihcet ohmen... Mon omat, momētis okis, kicvtēs.

Momen mv cvtoknawv cukpe-hvmke pale-cahkēpat, mv cerakko-cvlahet enfēkvtēs. Mohmen enrecapvtēs. Momen kohv-motkeu ēmvtēs. Momen mvn ēmet okat, Heyv kohv cēmvyat censumikats. Vcayēcet eshueretskvrēs, kihcet, ehmet ohmen, vyēpvtēs. Nǫksesekot vyēpvtēs.

Momen hvyatken mv cēpanat eratet rvlaken, cvpofv-pucaset em pohet okat, Naket noksekon hvyatkehaks? kicen... Naket nǫksesekon hvyatkes, kicet omen... Mon omat, ahyit erhēcin... Momēpet on omat, cvtoknawv cukpe-hvmke pale-cahkēpat cenfēkarēs, kihcet ayvtēs.

fire, and sat on the ground. And when he got sleepy, he made it so the pins were sticking all over a blanket, and he spread that out, pinpoints up, so when he fell asleep, he would fall on it, roll on it, wake himself, and continue to sit and wait.

Now as the night wore on, hearing a racket, he said, I've got you now! and when he got there, he saw it was a little spotted horse standing there as he approached.

And as soon as he got there, that spotted horse said, Set me free. I'll never eat crops again, he said to him... [The boy replied,] saying, I cannot set you free, not until the owner of the field sees you... How much are you going to be paid? he asked... I'm to be paid one hundred and fifty dollars ($150.00), he said... Well, then, I'll pay you the same, too. And wherever you go, I'll give you a reed whistle... If you keep it with you and think of me sometimes, I'll be with you, no matter what happens, I'll be with you, he promised him... Well, then, that would be all right, [the boy] said to him.

So the spotted horse paid him the one hundred and fifty dollars. Then he set him loose. And he gave him the reed whistle, too. And as he gave it to him, he said, You must not lose this reed I give you. You must take care of it, he said to him, and after giving it to him, [the horse] departed. He left without eating any of the crops.

And in the morning the boy returned, and the owner of the field asked him, Had nothing devoured my crops by dawn?... Nothing had devoured your crops by dawn, he said... Well, then, I'll go and see... If it is so, I'll pay you one hundred and fifty dollars, he said to him, and left.

Mont aret cvpofv eroret oman, mv nake noksvtē vketēcet aret oman, naket noksepekon okēpen aret yefulket erohret, mvn okvtētok, cvtoknawv cukpe-hvmke pale-cahkēpat mv cēpvnē mvnettat enfēkvtēs. Momen hvtvm mv cerakko-cvlahe ēmvtē 'somvlkat cvtoknawv cukpe tuccēnat ($300.00) em orēpvtēs.

Mohmen mv vtutketv pucase tat momusen, Nake erem ēti vtutketv ocepvkot onkv, hvtvm ētvn hopoyepvranatskat tvlket omēs. Momis enhvlwvn momylkusēn cehmvkin, fullet omatskvrēs, kihcet, momēn em etetakuecvtēs. Mohmen vpēyvtēs.

Vpēyet fullen, mv 'svculvkuecat okaket, Cēme tawvn cenhompet omēn, ecenahen omat, momusen hvtvm pome oceyan punhompetsken omvrēs, kicaken... Momētis os, kicet omet, hompetv mv cēpvnē yopv aran em papet enlokakvtēs. Mohmen mv cēpanat momusen hompetv vnahēpekv, mv ervhvlken enhompetvn eyacet oman, Punhompetskē taye onkot os. Momis ceturwv pvlhvmken cem ak-ēsēn omat tylkusan tąwvn punhompetskēs, kicaken... Mon omat, monkvn os, kihcen, turwv hvmken em ak-esahken enhompvtēs.

Mohmen hvtvm elawet oket, hvtvm em pohet omen... Okakat, hvtvm Pvlhvmkēn cem ak-ēsēn omat tylkusat tąwvn punhompetskēs, kicakvtēs. Momen em vkvsamvtēs. Mohmen em ak-esakvtēs. Mohmen mvn okakekv, hompicakvtēs.

Mohmen vpēyvtēs. Momis hęceseko hayakvtēs. Mon hecekon ēyvpayet eswelakvtēs. Mon esvhoyen okatet, Cekvn cem vhopotēcēt este-lvstucen cehayēn fullet omvkēs, kicaken... Momēs, kihcen, Mvo emvhopotecakvtēs. Mohmet este-lvste vhakēn hayet eswelakvtēs.

[The owner] reached the field, and when he checked around for that thing that had been eating crops, [he saw that] nothing had been eating crops, so he returned, and as he had said, he paid the young boy one hundred and fifty dollars. With everything that the spotted horse had given him, it amounted to three hundred dollars ($300.00).

Then the boss [said], I have no other work, so you must search elsewhere. But I will give you all equal provisions for your journey, he said to them, and made provisions for them. Then they departed.

As they were on their way, the older ones said, We'll eat yours first, and when you have no more, then you'll eat what we have, they said to him... Very well, he said to them, and they ate the youngest brother's food until they had eaten it up. Then when the boy had no more food, and wanted to eat the brothers' [food], [they said,] You can't eat with us. Only if we take out one of your eyes can you eat our food, they said to him... Well, then, do it, he said to them, and they took out one of his eyes and he ate of their food.

Then again he said he was hungry, and again he asked them [for food]... Again, they said, Only if we take out one of your [eyes] can you eat our food, they said. And he agreed. So they took his [other eye] out. Then because they had said that, they fed him.

Then they departed. But they had made him sightless. As he was blind, they took him about with them. As they were taking him, they said, Let's singe your head and make a black child of you as we go about, they said... All right, he said to them... They also singed him. Thus they made him look like a black person and took him about with them.

Mon eswelakof, Owvn cvwvnhkēs, kicen... Vsin uekiwvt liks. Mvn eskvs. Hvlket ayetskan, ocvrēs, kicaken, ayet uewv enkorkv sufkēt ocen okaken... Ayet erorof, vhepakkuehcet, mv uekiwv sufkan aakwikakvtēs. Momis elekot eraklatkvtēs. Mohmet vkerricat, mv kohv-mutken vkerricat vtękuset, aehset pofkan, eturwv hokkolvt ocē hakvtēs. Momen mv uekiwv onvpv mv cerakko-cvlahuce ēyohhuyiret eswvnakvn mv uekiwvn iem akkahyen, mv eswvnakvn vtvriket ohmen... Mv cerakko-cvlahet aak-ehsen, Tokvs. Vsin toknawv vhomkatat esohkakis. Monkv vcohlikvs. Assēcvkēts, kihcen... Momusen ohlihken esvlētkat, nenen ohwelaken oken erescakken ont omis, mv estvlke hokkolē welakat momēn heyv este-mvnettat momēn mv naket em vnican kerrvkekatēs. Momen okakat, Naket estomet oman, nake momē tayē onkot oman... Momēt arekv arekvn os, kicakvtēs. Momen hvtvm etohkvliket vpēyvtēs.

Momen vpēyet cuko ocēn eroricvtēs. Momen mv cuko epucasen em punayet okakat, Heyv este-mvnettan centaklicepetvn puyacet os, kicakvtēs. Momen okat, Momētis os, kicvtēs. Momen okakat, Estvn ravrēcihcetskvs, kicakvtēs. Momen, Momvrēs, kicvtēs. Mont vhoyēpvtēs.

Tvlofvn hoktē-vcąkēt likēt omvtēs. Moman estit mv hoktē enke-wesakvn estenke-wesakpikvn enke-wesakvn em piken omat, mv este mv momēcat mvt ēpvyvrēs, kihocēt omen, mvn eyacet welaket omvtēs. Momet mv momēcetv kont omakēto stomis momēceko tayvtēs.

Momen heyv este-mvnette cuko-pucase enwihokē taklikatet okatet, Ravretvn cvyacan onkv, vm etektvnehcetsken arit eracēyvyē tayēs, kicet, cuko-pucasen empohen... Cuko-pucaset okat, Estvn vrēcicekot

As they were leading him about, he said, I'm thirsty for water. Over there is a well. Drink there. As you crawl forward, it will be there, they said to him, and he went toward the deep well they were talking about... As he got there, they pushed him and threw him into that deep well. Though he fell down into it, he did not die. Then as he thought about it, he instantly remembered the reed whistle, took it out, blew it, and immediately had both eyes. And it happened that the little spotted horse stood at the top of the well and threw a rope down into the well, and [the boy] hung onto the rope... The spotted horse pulled him up, [saying,] Now! They were sitting over there counting the money. So sit upon me. Let's chase them, he said... Immediately he sat upon him and [the horse] sped off with him, catching up with them on the road, but the two boys didn't know that [the horse] had helped the youngest boy. And they said, Why is it, when it seems impossible, that he is here?... Just let him be, they said. And again they got together and started out.

As they were going they came to a house. And they spoke to the owner of the house, saying, We'd like to have this young man stay with you. And [the owner] said, It would be all right. And they said, Don't let him go anywhere. And he said, It will be so. Then the two departed.

In town lived a very elegant woman. Now it was said that whoever would be able to put a ring on the woman's finger would marry her, and they were desirous of that. And though they tried to do it, they could not do it.

Now the young man left in the care of the house owner spoke to him, saying, I need to go outside, so give me permission and I'll go and come back in, he said, asking the owner of the house... The owner of the house taklicetskvrēs, cvkicet okhohyekv, monkvs, cekicvko tayet ont on os, kicvtēs.

Momen mv este-mvnettat okat, Mon omat, yata cuko ofvn omvranvyat tvlkan omēs, cent oketskekv, kicof... Moman aret rafolotkepvs, kihcen, ossat momusen mv kohv-motken pofkvtēs. Momet mv kohv-motken vkerricat, momen nake estomēto stomis vcvpaket vm vnicvranet makvtēn ocvyēt omēs, kont vkerricat, mv cerakkot vlvkekvs, kohmet, pofkan vtękusen, mv cerakko-cvlahe tat momusen yenhuyiren... Ohlihket eslētkan, mv hoktē momē likat resohret eraslētkat, resvlahket yewiken cuko yecēyēpvtēs.

Momen mv cuko-pucase estvn ayet eratat kęrresekot liken, mv estvlke hokkolē welakat ravthoyet rvlahoket okakat, Estvn vrekathaks? kicet cuko-pucasen em pohakvtēs. Mon cuko-pucaset okat, Osiyet racēyvranis, maken, Moman momvs, kihcin, aret eraceyis, kicet em onayvtēs. Momen hvtvm tvlofvn yefulhoket omet okat, Mucv tat estvn vrekot takliket omvrēs, kicahket, hvtvm tvlofv vhoyepvtēs.

Mont min welakof, hvtvm mvn makat okekv, matvpomēn kicen, hvtvm em vkvsamvtēs. Mohmen ossat, hvtvm kohv-motke tat aehset pofkvtēs. Moman vtękusen hvtvm mv cerakko-cvlahe tat yenhuyiren, momusen ohlihket eslētkat 'sayet mv hoktē enke afvnecē likat estenke-wesakpikv herąkat enke-wesakv tat em pihket, resetehoyanet hvtvm raslētkat, mv cuko vhvoke-tempen yehvtvpecihcen, mv cuko ofv hoktē vcakē likat yecēyēpvtēs. Mont mv hoktē ēpvyēpvtēs.

said, I was told to keep you and not let you go anywhere, so I can't give you permission to do that, he said.

And the young man said, Well, then, I'll have to go here in the house, as you say... Well, go and come back, [the house owner] said, and having gone out, immediately he blew the reed whistle. And he thought of the reed whistle, and he thought, Whatever happens I have the promise it will be with me and help me, the horse must come, he thought, and as soon as he blew it, the spotted horse came and stood before him... He got on and raced the horse, arriving at the place where the woman lived, and [the horse] raced back and brought him to the house [where he was staying], and he went back inside.

Now the owner of the house sat not knowing that he had gone and returned, and the two boys who had been about came back: Did he not go anywhere? they asked the owner of the house. And the owner of the house said, He said he needed to go out and would come back in, and I told him, Very well, and he went out and came back in, he told them. And as they were going back to town again, they said, This time he's not to go anywhere, they said, and again they went to town.

And while they were there [in town], again [the youngest son] asked the same question, and again [the owner of the house] agreed. Then he went outside, and again taking the reed whistle out, he blew it. As soon as he did it, again the spotted horse came and stood before him, and as soon as he got on, he raced off with him, to where the girl with her hand held out for the ring lived, and he put the valuable ring on her finger, and as he raced by again, the horse let him off near the door of the house, and he went into the house where the elegant woman lived. And he got to marry the woman.

Momen, momēn mv hoktē ēpvyēpat kerrvkekot rvlahokvtēs. Momet sepekon rvlahohket yvpohakvtēs. Momen cuko-pucaset okat, Ravrvranis, maken, Momvs, kihcin, osiyat sepekon yomat oret os, kicen... Estvn estont omat kerretvn yacaket welaket vketēcakvtēs. Mont oman, mv hoktē vcąkē mahokē likvtē estenke-wesakpikv em piket mont ēpayet likēpvcoken kerrakvtēs. Mont mvn kerrakat, enhomecvkē tatēs. Momis estont estomvkeko tayet kerrakof momusen, Yefulhokepvkēs, kicahket yefulhokēpvtēs.

Mont welaket, erke-vcule likat rorhoyvtēs. Mont erken ennak onvyaket okakat, Ceppuce pucuse tat elehpen hēren vcayēceyvnks cē, kicet erke yenlaksakvtēs. Momen mv vculat okat, Enhopelkv tųlkusis hecēpvyēs. 'Svcvhohyatsken, kicet oman... Hopvyē hēret omēpekv ont on os, kicet, 'svhoyekatēs.

Momen mv este-mvnettat mv hoktē ēpahyof okatet, Tohahvwv tvnticvs, ehiwvn kicvtēs. Mon mvn okekv, tohahvwv ocat vtēkat omųlkvn tvnticvtēs. Mon Mvn okhoyvtēs, komat, kohv-motke tat aehset pofkvtēs. Toknawvt omekvs kohmet omat... Monkv mv kohv-motke pofkat, tohahvwv hvmken enramet mvn ohpofket omvtēs. Moman mvn kont onkv, cvtoknawv estomēt komvkat omvlkvt apvlatken, pofkvtēs. Mon mv tohahvwv fvciken, hvtvm ētvn matvpon momēcet omvlkvn fvcficvtēs. Mont hericet likępvtēs.

Momen ayen mv este mvnettusēt omvtētis, hofonēn mi hopvyēn liket este vculē haket, mont em enak ockv tis svmmomē-mąhēt enliketv herēn ocet liket omatet... Ehiwvn em punayet okat: Cvrket liken atvyvntvs. Estomvt'n omat hēcit arit... Mi vm ēkvnv ahyit arit erfulutketvn cvyacet os, kicen... Vneu cecak-vyarēs. Momēn welaket rvthoyeyvrēs, kicet omen, em vkvsamvtēs. Mon vhoyvtēs.

So it was that [the two brothers] returned not knowing he had married the woman. And because he was gone when they returned, they asked about him. And the owner of the house said, He said he wanted to go out, and I said, Very well, and he went out and has been gone up to now... Wanting to know where he went, they checked around. And so they learned that he had put the ring on the finger of the elegant woman and had married her. When they found out, they were furious with him. But when they realized they could do nothing, they said, Let's go home, and returned home.

And going about, they got to where their elderly father lived. Now they lied to their father, telling him, Your son, our brother, died and we buried him with respect. Then the old man said, If only I could see his grave. You two could take me, he said... It's very far, they said, and didn't take him.

And so it was that after the young man had married the woman, he said to his wife, Empty some boxes. And because he said that, she emptied all the boxes there. And thinking, This is what [the horse] meant, he took out the reed whistle and blew it. Let it be money, he thought... So as he blew on the reed whistle, he opened a box and blew on it. And as he wished, he saw all kinds of money spilling out, and he blew again. And that box filled up, and again he did the others the same way and filled all of them. And he stored it all away and sat back.

As time went on, though he had been a very young man, he had lived for a long time far away and had become an old man, and he had become a possessor of valuable things and lived in a fine home... He spoke with his wife: My father was alive when I came here. I'm going to go see what happened to him... I want to go to my country, be there awhile, and return, he said... I, too, will go with you, [she said]. We'll go and come back like that, he said, and she agreed. So they went.

Welaket erke likat erorhoyvtēs. Momen mv erke encuko rorhoyat, momusen Fēkvpepaks, kicvtēs. Momis momē mv eppuce resyupv arvtēt omat kẹrresekatēs. Momen mv ervhvlket cerakko em vcayēcaks, erket kihcen, corakko-huten 'svhoyet, corakkon enrecvprēcet welaken, hvmket okat, Mv este estit os kontska? kicen... Kerrvkot os, kicof... Pucuse omat os. Monkv hiyomusen tokorkepvkēs, kihcen, sumhokēpvtēs.

Mon mv este-mvnette sumkvtē erke tat kẹrresekot takliket omen em pohvtēs. Mon em ēyonayvtēs. Mon kērrvtēs. Ohletiket, vfvnket 'sarvtēs. Mon estomēcē eswelakvtē omylkvn em onayet respoyof, Mv estvlke hoporrenkv ocvkekot omvttis. Pvsvtvkēs, kicahket ont omis, sumhokēpen estomēcekatēs. Mon sumhokemahēpvtēs.

Going there, they arrived at the place where his father lived. And when they reached his father's house, he immediately told them to rest. Yet he didn't know that [the man] was his youngest son. Now the father told the brothers to take care of their horses, and they took them to the barn and were going about untying the horses when one said, Who do you think that person is? I don't know, the other said... He used to be our brother. So let's run away right now, he said, and they disappeared.

And the father still did not recognize the young man who had been lost, and [the son] asked him [if he knew] who he was. And he told him all about himself. And then [the father] knew. He ran to him, kissed him, and led him around. Then [the son] told him how the two brothers had treated him, and as he finished, [the father said,] Those people must have had no sense, then. Let's kill them, they said, but they had vanished, and they could do nothing. And they disappeared for good.

2

The hunter and his dogs

A sick man has a wife who beats his dogs and is away a great deal. The oldest dog convinces him to take all the dogs hunting by traveling in a boat. They kill a bear, then discover the wife with a man in a field house and punish them. The dogs get the man to visit a house where a young woman lives. The dogs understand and obey her, and she becomes the man's wife (cf. Swanton (1929), Creek story 18).

Stories 2, 4, and 19 develop the character of the old dog and the special role he plays as advisor to his master. The dogs in this story punish the adulterous wife and find a replacement who understands them.

Heyvt fakvn ayesasvtēt omet os cē.

Este hvmket enokkēt wakkvtēs. Momet ehiwv ocēt omvtēs. Momet hvtvm efvn sulkēn ocēt omvtēs.

Momen mv este-honvnwv tat, ehiwvt mv este-honvnwv enokkan ennaoret arvtēs. Momet mv efvo 'somylkvn enhomecētut ont, efv tat nvfketekayet mv hoktēt 'sarvtēs. Mont sumkēpat vrēpen, yafken rvlaket, mv hoktē arēt omvtēs.

Momen nettv hvmken mv hoktē sepekon yvfkvranet omen mv efv vpokat hvmket omylkv 'sem vculēt vpvkēt omvtēs. Mont omvtētan, mv efv-vculet mv este enokkan aoh-ahtet em punayvtēs. Mont okat, Cehiwv tat cennaoruset vrēpet ont, pomeu 'somylkeyan punhomecepēt omētt os. Mont on mvnettvlket okakat, Fakvn 'sepoyēs, makaket os, kicet mv efv-vculet em onayvtēs, epucasen. Mont okat, Yvkapit vrvko tayuset omēpekv, estohmvkos, kicvtēs. Momen efv-mvnettvlke em onayin, estos, makvkvrēs, kihcet omet, eriem onayen, Punt 'svpeyeyvrēs, makaken... Hvtvm Momēn makaks, kicet yem onayvtēs. Mont, Nake esfayē 'svrvkē tayat punt 'sem vpeyvranet okēs, kicakvtēs. Moman momvranen omēs kicvtēs.

Moman perron ocēt omvtēs, mv este-honvnwv enokkat. Mon hvcce vwolusēt omvtēs. Momen mvn okakekv, momusen eccv tis, rē-hotvwv tis iesentak-ocen, momusen efv tat mvn coksakket 'svpēyet, mv perro ervtehhet, mont nake esnoricvkē tayatto 'stomis omylkvn efvt takuecvtēs. Perron ervtehhet, mohmet epucasen hvtvm 'svpeyetvn kicakvtēs.

Mont okakat, Cem etetakekvs. Vccetvn ohwakkvs, kicahken, momusen ohwakkvtēs. Mohmen efvt mv vccetv em vtēkēn em akkē vlket, eskvwahpet 'svpeyēpvtēs.

This is about someone who went hunting.

A man lay sick. And he had a wife. And he also had many dogs.

Now the man's wife was tired of the sick man. She was annoyed with all the dogs, too, and would go around beating them. Now the woman would disappear for long periods, returning in the evening.

One day the woman was gone and it was getting late, and among the dogs there was one older than the others. And the old dog came up to the sick man and spoke to him. And he said, Your wife is annoyed with you and angry at all of us as well. And the young ones keep saying, He could take us hunting! the old dog told his master. And [the man] replied, Because I am unable to walk, I can't do anything. Then [the dog said], I'll tell that to the young ones and see what they say, and he went and told them and they said, We'll take him... Again [the dog] came and told him, Here's what they said. They said, We'll take everything needed for hunting. Well, then, let it be done, [the man] said.

Now the sick man had a boat. And the river was very close. And because they meant what they said, immediately he put his gun and shot pouch on the floor, and immediately the dogs put them in their mouths, took them, and put them in the boat, and prepared all the utensils needed for cooking. They put them in the boat, then they told their master they'd take him next.

And they said, It's ready for you. Lie on the quilt, they said to him, and immediately he lay on it. Then with all of the dogs biting the edges of the quilt, they lifted it and carried him.

Mont perro ocat eresoricvtēs. Mont erohpikvkēpvtēs. Momusen ohwvkiken 'sak-vpēyvtēs. Mv este enokkat ohwakkusēt perro kafen 'svpēyvtēs.

Momen efv vcule-mahat mvt vpakvtēs. Momen erem ētv sulkēt onkv, mvt lvpvtkēn vpēyet, fayet vpēyvtēs.

Mon mv lvpvtkē fayē vpēyat, ero tis, kono tis, nake hompvkē tayat vtēkat elēcet resyicet mv perron yem ohtēhet, sulkēn hayaken perro ervc-cayvtēs. Mont mvn enokkuset omēpekv, ont omis lvpvtkē osset omis, mata hvcce-vfopken wakken, efv ētvt eto hopoyet sulkēn enhopoyakvtēs. Momen mvn 'tēcvtēs. Vkecattueckv ocvtet totkv 'tēcet omet, mv efv fayakat tat momusen hvsvthicet, mont efvo hompicet, ēmeu hompet tak-likēpvtēs.

Mont ohhvyvtiken, hvtvm vpēyvtēs. Mont omvtētok matvpomēn hvtvm vpēyat, hvtvm erfekhonnen, hvtvm matvpomēn mēcvtēs. Momēcet 'svpēyet fakv ēkvnv komat roricvtēs.

Mont ervpoken, mv este enokkē esfullvtē mv tis vrēpusē erenhakēpen, efv afvckvkē hēret fullen... Mv esteu nake elēcvt omvtētis omvtētok, momusen mv este tat eco tis elēcet omen... Hvtvm mv efv-vcule tat mv este em onayet okat: Nokosen entohkvranet omēkv em ehakē tayen omat mvn em pohvs, makaket os, kicet em onayen... Mv vtēkusat vrvyē tayuset omis os, kihcen... Momusen efv tat vpeyēpvtēs. Mon mv efv-vcule tat mv epucase tat vpaken kaken, efv-mvnettvlke tat vpēyet omētat... Efv tat saksakusat tut omen, momusen nokose tat hecvkē hēret omvcoks, maket mv efv pucaset 'tepaket kaken... Ayen momusen yvwo-licet vyēcicen, kaken... Esfullet esyicat, nokose rakkē hēren esfullet

In this way they got to where the boat was. And they put him in. Immediately he lay down and they took off. The sick man rowed the boat while lying down as they took him.

Now the oldest dog was with him. And because there were many others, they hunted on shore as they went.

Now those that were hunting on shore killed squirrel, skunk, and anything that one could eat, and they would return and put them in the boat in such great quantities that he had to land the boat. Even though he was sick, he went ashore and lay near the edge of the river, and the other dogs searched for wood and gathered a great deal for him. With that he built a fire. Having a flint, he lit the fire, cleaned what the dogs had hunted, fed some to the dogs, and then ate some himself and sat back.

Now the next day they moved on. Just as before, they went, and he stopped again and did the same thing each time. They traveled in this way until they reached the desired hunting ground.

While staying there, the sick man they'd brought had begun to get around a little, and the dogs were very happy... The man had once been a hunter, and was ably killing deer... Now the old dog told the man: [The young dogs] say, We're going to drive a bear, so ask if he can lie in wait! Surely I can do that much, [the man] said... Immediately the dogs left. The old dog and his master sat together, while the young dogs started out... The lively yelping of the dogs surely means they've seen a bear, he said, and the dog and his master sat together and waited... Then after a while they came closer, and they waited... As they came, they saw they'd brought a great big bear... Then as he was about to kill it... Wait. Wait a ohkvtet esyicet omen... Momusen elēcvranet omen... Hvtēc. Mucv hvtvm estomosis ayusē monket maken, 'svpēyet este-hvpo resvwolicen... Tokvs! Elēcvnos! kicahken, em elēcvtēs. Momen mvn tayē hērnen hompakvtēs.

Mont tak-vpoken, efv tat epucasen em punayet okat, Cehiwv tat hiyomat este-honvnwv heckuecet cvpof-cukon eslumhet omhos. Monkv, Vhakv vfvstvkēs, kont maken omat, vfvsteyē tayet omēs, makaket onkv, estos kontsken okaken omat, kicen... Estos kont okaken omat mēcvkvranat tvlkēs, kihcet, em vkvsamvtēs.

Mohmen mv efv-mvnettvlke tat momusen em etetahket momusen vpēyvtēs. Mont hvt-vpēyat tat pohkv hēren wohokakat pohkv hēren wohoket... Hvtvm wohokat estomuset pohken erwohokaket... Hvtvm kohmē erwohokakat pohkē orosekon erwohokat sumecēpvtē... Hvtvm hvyvtkvranes komvkē haken hvtvm estomuset pohken wohokaket omen... Momusen erawē hērvcokis os, maket mv efv-vcule tat totkv pvl-hvmken atakwakken... Takkaken ayen hvtvm wohokakat pohkvn hēren hvtvm wohokaken... Mucv tat yicē hērvcokis os, maken, takkaken eryicvtēs. Mont eryicat, Cukhvce tat catv-vlhēkuset eryicvntvs, make-sasvtēs, maket onahoyvntvs.

Mohmen okakat: Cvpof-cukon wakhokēpvten erorihcēt vhakv tat esv-fasteyvnks, maket eryicvtēs. Momen tak-vpoket omatet ervwepvranet omen, efvt, okakat, Hiyomē yefulecvraneyat, esepoyet, este hvmket likēt omen kerrvkēt ont omet, mv este encukon resepuretskvrēs kicakvtēs.

Momen mvn okakvtētok, mv cuko okakaten eresorvtēs. Mont hvte mv cuko resoreko monkof okat: Mv cuko roricēn omat, mv cuko vpokat cen nak onayet okakat, Hoktē licetskvnkē tat em vkerrickv kucōknusēt omvtet este-honvnwv enheckēt liket os, mahoken pohvkēt omētvnken...

little longer, [the old dog] said as they neared the camp... Now! Kill him! they said, and he killed it for them. And they ate a great deal.

Now as they were sitting around, the dog told his master, Your wife has found a man and they are lying in the field house. The young dogs are saying, If he says to apply the law, we will carry it out, so whatever you think of what they're saying, [we'll do, the dog] said... Whatever they think, they should do it, [the man] agreed.

Then the young dogs immediately got ready and started out. And as they started out, the howling was loud and clear, the howling was very clear... Now the howling was becoming distant... Again as they howled it was very faint until they were heard no more... Then just about daybreak, the howling could be heard faintly in the distance... Now they're coming back, the old dog said, lying on the other side of the fire as they waited... After a while the howling could be heard again loud and clear, as they howled... Surely they're almost here, he said as they sat, and they arrived back. When they arrived, the corners of their mouths were covered with blood, someone once said, they used to tell.

Then [the dogs] said: We arrived where they were lying together in the field house and administered the law. Then they sat awhile and as they were about ready to leave for home, the dogs said: Now that we're going back, take us to where a man we know lives, take us to the man's house.

And just as they'd requested, he took them to that house. And just before they reached the house, [the dog] said: When we get to that house, those living in the house will tell you, We heard it said that the woman you kept had a very short memory and that she found a man and is living

Nerē-fullvt yvmahkuecēpvcokvnks, maket cem onahoyvrēs. Mahoken omēto 'stomis, Momēpvt tis, maketskan vtẹkusvrēs, cvkicakvntvs, make-sasvtēs, mahokvnts.

Mon fullẹtt eryicvtēs. Momen mvn okakvtētok, mv efv nake makē em onvyakvtē mạhusan momvtēs. Momen hvtvm okakat, Hompetv cenhopo-hoyat oketskat, Efv mit vm elvwạkusen 'sarit omis, maketskvrēs. Mont Efv mit homp[vk]ekvs, mahket cvtvhakvn vtēwv facken iescenwvkec-hoyvrēs.

Momof, Efv mit hompvkekvs mahket iespum wvkehcetsken puntạt hom-peyvrēs. Momof yopvn hompepetskvrēs.

Momen cennak onvyaket okat, Hoktē tat honvnwv heckuecēt omvnken, nerē-fullvt yvmahkuecētt omvcokvnks, makaket, mont ēmeu hvkihhoket esfulleto 'stomis, Momvt tis maketskan vtẹkusvrēs. Cvkicakvtē mv mạhusan momvranen okvkēpvten, momvntvs, makesasvtēs, mahokvnts.

Momen mv cuko erorat, vyeko monket okat, Vsi hvccen perrot akwakkēs. Mvn vpeswv 'stomusat ocēt omētok eracawet noricet hompepaks, kicen... Rahechoyan vpeswv estọmēt komvkat, mvn perro facket 'sakwakken oken, vpeswv tat rehcahwet, noricet, hompet vpohoken oman... Efvt mv cuko este vpokat hoktē-mvnette hvmken lihocēt oman, mv efv mv este ēyvpvyē 'sarvtē, mv hoktē mvnettan, efvt em ahkopanet esfullet omen... Mv hoktēt okat, Momē hayekot vpeswv tis resawet vsi vce-hute tis yvte-hetvts, kican... Momusen mv momē kihocan vtẹkusen mv efv tat pefatket, momusen vpeswv resyicet, vce-hute tat resvtasēcet ervtēhet, momēcet esfullẹpen... Mv cuko vpoket okat, Estomen momēt efvt fullet omehaks? kihocen... Mv hoktē-mvnettat okat, Vnet okit, efvt vm ahkopanet fullet omen okvyat, Momē hayekot vpeswv tis resawet vsi vce-hute tis yvte-

with him... The coyotes did away with her, they'll tell you. But when they say that, All you will answer will be, And so they did, they told me, someone once said, it was told.

They finally returned. And as they had said, it happened just as the dog had said. And now they said, When they're preparing food for you, you will say, I have very hungry dogs with me. And say, Let the dog[s] eat first, and they will place a winnowing-basket full of blue bread before you.

When that happens, say, Let the dogs eat first, and place it before us, and we will eat. When that happens, you will eat last.

And they will tell you things, saying, The woman found a man, but coyotes did away with her, they said, and even though they go around crying, you must say only, And so they did. Exactly what [the dogs] told me would happen, happened, someone has said, it was said.

And reaching that house, before he left, he said [to those living there], There's a boat down on that river. There's a little meat there. Go and get it, cook it, and eat it, he said... When they went to look, the boat lay there full of every imaginable kind of meat, and they got the meat, cooked it, and sat eating it... There was a young girl who lived in the home, and the dogs that the man had with him began playing with the young girl... The girl said to them, Instead of playing around, you ought to bring the meat and put it in the corncrib... As soon as she said that, the dogs ran, and immediately brought the meat, and jumping up into the corncrib, put the meat in the crib... When the people who lived there saw this, they asked, Why are the dogs doing this? The young girl said, I told them... The dogs were just playing around with me and I said, Quit playing around like

hetvt omes, kicvyan, efvt punvkv kȩrrakusē omēt omēpen ohkvyvten...
Mv nak kicvyat mahusan fullet os, makvtēs, mahokvnts.

Mohmen estonhkotok momusen mv este-honvnwv, mv hoktē-mvnette
lihocvtēt enwihoken... Mv este-honvnwv ehiwv enfvcceko, ehiwv nerē-
fullv enyvmahkuecē arat... Mvn hoktē tat momusen enheciken likepvra-
nen omēs kihohcen... Mv este momusen mvn ehisēpvtēs. Fakv arē
rvlakat vtȩkuset hoktē tat enheciken momusen fekhonnehpet likēpvtēs,
mahokvnts.

that and bring the meat and put it in the corncrib over there, and as I said
this, the dogs clearly understood my words... They are doing exactly
what I said, she said, it was said.

Then the man could not do anything when the young girl was given him
to be his wife... Now it was the man whose unfaithful wife had been done
away with by the coyotes... This is how they gave him the girl, saying, I
guess he can settle down now... So the man took her as his wife. As soon
as he returned from the hunting trip, he found a woman and immediately
settled down, it's been said.

3

Tug-of-war between tie-snakes

Rabbit separately invites two tie-snakes to have a tug-of-war with him, giving each the end of a grapevine. After the two snakes battle each other, they discover the trick and ban Rabbit from drinking their water. He dresses up as a fawn so he can drink and they discover this, too. One day he finds a figure of tar on the riverbank. He fights it and gets stuck, and he's put in a box over the river. Wolf comes by, and Rabbit tells him he must eat three hogs or be thrown in the river. Wolf takes his place and is thrown in the river. After a long time, Rabbit reappears and tells of an exciting underwater town with many women. Many wish to go and are thrown in the water. Opossum wants to go so badly he searches in the cold water until his tail is withered (cf. Swanton 1929, Creek stories 49–53, 75, 77).

Here Rabbit shows mastery of estakwvnayv *'tie-snake', a powerful underwater snake. In this version, Earnest Gouge blends the story of a tug-of-war between tie-snakes with the tar-baby motif. In bringing up the opossum at the end, he anchors the story to an aspect of the world around us.*

Mohmen hvtvm cufet arvtēs, mahokvnts. Cufet uewvn ēsket arēt omvtēs.

Momen momvtētan hvcce kololokēt omen estvmi-vlkis uewv lvolvkē vlkēt ocet on omen, mvn mv cufe tat eskēpet, vrēpet omvtētut, estakwvnayvt akkakē vlkēt omen kerrvtēs.

Momet okat, mv cetton em punayet okat, Pvrko-fvkvn etenhvlvtēpvkēs, hvmken erkicen okat... Kos! Cvyekcē hẹrēt omēs. Cvstomehcetskekos, kicet oman... Momis vnet okikv, 'tenhvlatvkēs, kicen... Momētis okis, kicvtēs.

Momen hvtvm hvmken mvo matvpomēn rehkicen... Mvo, okat, Cvyekcē hẹrēt omēs. Cvstomehcetskekos, kicen... Momis vnet okikv, kicen... Momvranan omēs, kihcet ohmen... Mon omat, pvrko-fvkv hopohyin mvtarēs, kihcet, ayat pvrko-fvkv hopoyet aret pvrko-fvkv-cvpkon hopoyehpet... Momusen mv uewv eraktekkekēn erakwvkehcet, hvtvm ayat, hvtvm mv estakwvnayv hvmke aklikat mvo matvpomēn mv pvrko-fvkv erem akwvkehcet okatet... Pvrko-fvkvn nekēyicet, pihkin omat, momusen hvlatvyat okarēs, kihcet... Eratat hvtvm hvmken mvo rem ohret mvo matvpomēn, kicen... Mon omat, momvrēs, kihcen, ayat mvn okekv estvmi-vlkis hokkolvn momēn kicekv, momusen mv pvrko-fvkv nvrkvpvn ahyet, momusen erennekēyihcet momusen pihket omen... Hvlvtē hẹret okēs, komat, momusen estvmi-vlkis hvlvtakvtēs.

Mohmet here-mahen etenhvlatet... Pvrko-fvkv tat wekekēckē haken 'sakkakēpen... Cufe tat pihket, tafv-hvtkuce 'kvcakhēcet, mv pvrko-fvkv 'tenhvlvtē wvkechoyat nvrkvpvn vfvtosket ahkopanat vhvrēpvtet, letiket ayat hvcce erohfvnket erhēcan... Mv cetto tat yossicē omvnton, hvtvm

And now it was said there was once a rabbit. The rabbit would go about drinking water.

Now the river twisted and was flooded everywhere, and the rabbit would go about drinking there and learned that two tie-snakes were always down there.

And addressing the snakes, he went and told one, Let's have a tug-of-war with a grapevine... No! I'm very strong. You won't be able to handle me, [the snake] said... But I'm the one who wants to, so let's have a tug-of-war with one another, he said... Well, all right, [the snake] said.

Then he went and told the other the same thing... That one, too, said, I'm very strong. You won't be able to handle me, he said... But I'm the one who wants to, [Rabbit] said... Then let it happen, [the snake] said... Well, then, I'll look for a grapevine and that will be it, he said, and from there he went about looking for a grapevine and found a long grapevine... Then he laid one end down touching the water's edge, and moving on again, he laid it out in the same way where the other tie-snake was... When I move the grapevine and whoop, that will mean I'm pulling, he said... Coming back, he reached the other one, and told that one the same thing, too... Well, then, let it happen, [the snake] said, and going on, having said it to each of them, [Rabbit] went to the middle of the grapevine and shook it and whooped... He must have a really good hold, they both thought, and each side began to pull.

Then they began to have a good pull... The grapevine began to creak, but they kept at it... Rabbit whooped, wearing a little white feather on his head, and he jumped around at the middle of the grapevine that was stretched out, and played awhile, then he'd run to the edge of the river

yesvlētken hēcet rohhuervtētut... Ralētkat, hvtvm 'tehoyanat, hvtvm
hvmken rehhēcan... Mvo matvpomēn mvo yossicē omē haken, hvtvm
yesvlētken... 'Sakkaket on, estvmi-vlkis rehhēcet 'sem etoh-aret, vpelicet
vrēpen... Kot, Cufet omatet, momvtēken yekcētut omehakes? estakwvnayv hvmket kohmet... Yohfvniket hēcan, Cufe tat naken hvlvtekot
ahkopvnēt vrēpen eshēcvtēs. Mohmet ēme-vlken mv pvrko-fvkv etenhvlatet omat erkerrakvtēs.

Mont momusen okakat, 'Svnvcomv uewv pum eskekot aret omvrēs,
kicakvtēs. Momen Cufe tat vyēpvtēs.

Mont vrēpet omatet, ecuce hvrpe tokohusvnton vciyet, momusen ayvtēs.
Aret uewv ocat eroret okat, Uewvn vm encahokēt omēpvcoket ont omis,
arit omis, kicet omen... Centokon—Pasokolvyvn okhoyvtēt omēs, kihocen, momusen uewv tat esiket vyēpvtēs. Mont vrēpet omvtēs. Momen
ayen mvt Pasokolvyvt aret ont omis okēpē ont omat, ayen
erkerrohoyvtēs.

Mont omet, nake este-vhaken colokcowvt este hayvkvtēn hvcce vfopken
enhuerihocen momusen erorvtēs. Mont, Uewvn cem eskvranis cē! kicen
ont omis, mvn wenakekot omēpekv, nak makeko tayet huerēpen... Oh-
ahyet, Cenvfkarēs vm punvyetskeko tayen omat, kicet omis, Mvn
wenakepekok em punvyekot omēpen... Momusen nafkvtēs. Nafkan, enke
esnafkan vlokpvtēs. Momen, Cvwikvs. Hvtvm cvnke pvlhvmket vhoskēt
os. Mvn escenafkin omat, celēcarēs. Monkv elkvn ceyacekon omat,
cvwikvs! kicen ometo 'stomis, mvn colokcowvt omēpekv, naken
makekot omēpen... Mvn okekv enke pvlhvmkat hvtvm esnafkvtēs.
Momen mvo matvpomēn vlokpēpvtēs. Mon hvtvm cvlet vhoskēt os.
Mvn 'secohrēfkin omat, celēcarēs. Monkv cvwikvs! kican, wikeko

and look over the edge... He'd stand over them and watch a snake almost
get pulled out and then pull itself back in... He'd run back past again, going
to see the other one... That one, too, was almost getting pulled out of the
water the same way and pulling itself back in... They kept at it, and he'd
go back and forth checking on either side, all the while laughing at them...
Gosh, he's only a rabbit, can he be so strong? one tie-snake thought... When
he peered over [the bank], he found Rabbit playing around, not pulling
anything. Then they realized they alone had been pulling the grapevine.

Then they said, He will never again go about drinking our water. So Rabbit went away.

Now as he was wandering about, he draped himself in a little speckled
fawn hide and left. From there he reached the water, saying, They have
forbidden me water, but I am here anyway... Not you—we meant
Pasokolaya (Trickster Rabbit), [the tie-snakes] said, and then he drank
the water and went off. He did this regularly. And time passed, and they
suspected it was Pasokolaya, and later knew for certain.

One day, he came upon a figure made of tar that they had placed on the
riverbank. And he said, I'm going to drink your water! but it had no life
and so stood there unable to say anything... He went up to it: I will hit
you if you won't talk to me, he said, but it had no life and did not talk to
him... Then he hit him. When he hit him, the hand he hit him with got
stuck. Let go of me, he said. I still have my other hand. If I hit you with
that, I'll kill you. So if you don't want to die, let go of me! he said, but
because it was tar, it said nothing... Because he meant it, he hit him with
his other hand. And that one got stuck just like the other one. Well, I still
have my foot. If I kick you with that, I'll kill you. So let go of me! he
said, but it wouldn't let go... Again when he kicked him, that, too, got

tayen... Hvtvm ohrēfkan, mvo vlokpēpvtēs. Mon hvtvm cvle pvlhvmket vhoskēt os, kicen ont omis, nak makepekot huerēt omēpen... Hvtvm ele pvlhvmkan hvtvm esohrēfkan, mvo vlokpehpen okatet, Cvkvt vhoskēt os. Mvtat estomēto 'stomis celēcarēs. Monkv cvwikvs! kicet omis, mvn colokcowvt omēpekv, eshuerēpen, eshehcet, mv cufe tat eshoyvtēs.

Mont em vfvsitet 'senfvccēcat, 'Tohahvwvn vpihket 'semohrahrihcet, uewvn asakwikvkēs, kihocvtēs.

Mont mvn momēcvranet 'senfvccēcet omhoyekv, momusen 'tohahvwv tat 'sem ohcakcvhehcet, hvcce-onvpv resohlihocen... 'Sohlikof, Yvhvt erorvtēs. Mont okat, Vnhessē! Eston momēt liketska? kicen... Kot, Sukhv tuccēnan loketskekan heyv uewvn iecekwikvranet omēs! cvkihocet ont oman, lokepvko tayet omēpekv, heyv uewvn avcakwihokvranat tvlkuset omen liket omis, kicet omen... Okat, Cēmen cenwihkin, cent loketskēs, kicet omen... Mon omat, momepekvs. Vnet omarēs. Monkv, osiyet ontsken, vne mit ceyiyin, vm ohranvs, kihcen... Mi Yvhv mit mv 'tohahvwv tat ceyiyen, Cufe tat ossehpet momusen Yvhv min mv 'tohahvwv 'sem ohcakcvhehcet vyēpen... Mv uewv asakwikvranē fullvtē erorihcet, momusen asakwikvranet omhoyen... Vne mv toyaks! Mv to-yaks! mākusen, asakwihokvtēs.

Mohmen vyēpen hofonē haken, nvkaftet vpohoken... Cufet on omat vheckvtēkat eroren, mv este nvkaftē kakat hecakvtēs. Mont okakat, Pasokolvyv vnna arēt omētatet ervlaket os, kicet, vrakkuehocē hēren likvtēs. Mont nake onvkv ocē hēret omēs. Monkv punnak onvyekvs, kihocen liket... Okat, Mont os. Hiyomat mv momē uewv acakwihokvtē ayvyat, ayvyisan mv hvcce aknvrkvpv erorvkan nen-vpaske-rakkot vlvkēt omvten... Mvn ayvyat ayit omvyisan, este vpokēn erorvyvtēt os. Momen afvcketv estomēt komvkat, mvn omvlkvt ocepēt omēpen...

stuck. Well, I still have my other foot, he said, but it just stood there not saying anything... When he kicked again with his other foot, that, too, got stuck, and he said, I still have my head. No matter what, I'll kill you. So let go of me! he said, but it was tar, so it just stood there, and they found him stuck to it and caught the rabbit.

And after taking him to court and sentencing him, they said, Let's put him in a box, hammer him in, and throw it into the water.

Because they had sentenced him, right away they nailed him in the box and placed it up on the riverbank... While it was sitting there, Wolf came up. My friend! he said, Why are you sitting there? Well, they told me that if I don't eat three hogs, they'll throw me into the water, but I can't eat [that many], so they'll just have to throw me in the water, and that's why I'm sitting here, he said... But I could leave it to you, and you could eat them, he said... Well, then, let it be. I'll do it. So, you get out and I'll get in instead, and you put the lid over me, he said... Wolf got in the box instead, and Rabbit got out and nailed the box shut with Wolf in it and left... The ones who were to throw it in the water arrived, and were about to throw it in... Just as [Wolf] yelled, I'm not the one! It's not me! they threw it in.

Then after a long time they were sitting in a meeting... Rabbit came up in plain sight, and the people assembled saw him. And they said, Pasoko-laya from long ago has returned, and he sat with their utmost respect. He surely has a lot to tell. So let him tell us these things, they said as he sat... Yes, he said. When they threw me in the water like that I was leaving, but as I was going, as I reached the middle of the river, a big road came really close... As I was leaving, I took this [road] and reached a place where people lived. And they had all kinds of attractions there... They

Pokkechetvt komvkat, mv tawvt hoktvke tateu ehe svkekot tayēt omēpekv estehiwvt sekot on omat estehitake sulketo 'stomis vrēpvkēt ont omen... Yvmv tat ravkerricvkē tayē onkot, mvt tvlwv hērēt ocēt os. Mont omen mvn rorit omikv, mvn vrēpit omvyētvnket omis, Arit ervtarēs, mahket eratit omis, maket likvtēs, mahokvnts.

Mon este tat eyacakat, Vnet vyarēs! maken... Momusen 'tohahvwvn vtehhet mv uewv tat este sulkēn 'svpvlvthoyvtēs. Momen 'svnvcumvn heckv sekot s[u]mēcen, momusen vpohokē saset omen... Momusen Cufe tat mv uewv aksumiket mv nene ak-ocē makat, mvn ayē omēt... Ayat, mv uewv aksumkē ayat ak-vhopvyēn erossepvntut vrēpvtet... Hvtvm mv uewv aksumkētat eratat mv hvteceskv aksumkvtē mahusat yvfvnkvntut, yosset nake onayet arvtēs.

Mont okat, Yvmv este fullē vpēyatut on omat, estofvn yvmv eravkerricē tayē tokot vpokēs. Ehitake tis tuccēnet, monkat hvtvm ostis ocvkēpekv, estohmen yvmv tat ravkerricē tayē tokot vpokēs. Momet netta omylkvn pokkechetvt, momen opvnkvt afvcketv estomē vtēkat omvlkepvt omēpen fullēpēt os. Monkv este estomēto 'stomis mv etvlwv erorēto vtēkat erv-woskvranat tylkusēt omēpekv... Estofvn esti tat eratet vreko tayet ont omis, vntat 'svm ērolopkv omēcicēn eratet 'toh-arit omis, maket mv tat nake onayet aret omen... Momusen sukhv-hatkvt mvn vyetvn eyacet aret ehvswvn hokkolēn hayet arvtēs. Mv hoktvke estohmē 'setetahoyeko tayan mvn ayin omat, cvhitake sulkēn likvyē tayet etvlwv tat ocet omv-coks, kont... Momusen mv etvlwv ohnene hopoyvtēs. Mont mv uewv tat aksumkvntut, uewv ofv akyvkapet, etetiket, nenen hecetvn eyacet onkv vwicēcekot... avktaske-mahvtēs. Momet kvsvppēto 'stomis akhvtapket omen... Mv uewv akkvsvppē ak-arat omēcicēn mv sukhv-hatkv ehvce enkvsappēt [omēs], maket onahoyvnts cē. Monkv hoktvke eyackv omēcicēn ehvce tvlēcet omvtēs.

wanted to play ball and there were lots of women, unmarried women, so that if one were single, one could go around with many wives... One cannot even think back to this place, it is so exciting. So it was that I arrived there, and spent quite some time there, but I said, I'll go back, and came back, he said, sitting there, they used to say.

And the people who wanted to go there said, I'll go!... So they put them in a box and threw many people in the water. And they were never seen again, though some were still there... So Rabbit would disappear into the water saying there was a road there, as though he were going on it... And he would go far under the water and come out way downstream... Again, under water, he'd return to the exact spot where he had gone under, come out, and tell about his experiences.

And he said, The people who left from here can't even remember this place. Because they have three or even four wives, they're not even thinking of this place. And every day there are ball games, and dances, and all kinds of fun for those who are there. So no matter who you are or what town you're from, this place attracts everyone... Whenever someone comes there they cannot leave again, but because of my stubbornness, I go back and forth, he said as he went about... Then there was an opossum who decided to go there, so he made himself two penises. If I go to this place where there are more than enough women to go around, I can have many wives in a town like that, he thought... Then he looked for the road to the town. He would disappear into the water, and walk under water to the other side, and kept jumping in, not giving up because he wanted to find the road... And even though the water was cold, he stayed in it... It's because he was in that cold water so long that the opossum's tail is cold, they say. So it's because of a desire for women that his tail has become withered.

4

The hunters' wives

Two men go hunting. When men go hunting, they are told not to think back on their homes. During the night, two women appear who look just like their wives. An old dog warns one hunter that they're not their real wives, that he should poke one with a burning stick. When he does, it turns out to be a female fox. The other hunter snuggles up with what appears to be his wife. The first hunter is awakened by the sound of chomping bones and finds his friend has been killed. He escapes with his dogs, who hide the man in a hollow log when an owl tries to get him. The man is able to return home, but the two women are still out there today.

This is a scary story about estekene, *who change shape from humans to owls and other animals. Margaret Mauldin sees the old dog as representing the men's conscience or fidelity. Dogs have a similar role in story 2.*

Este hokkolet fakvn vhoyvtēs. Mont welaket ehvpo mahhe tat erhayet takkakvtēs. Momen momē fayvlke fullat okēpat, Est' encuko ēyvkerrihcēskos, maket hofonof fullet omvtēs. Mont oman, mv hvmkat tat pohyvkepē ont vrēpet omen... Kos. Momēt vretv tokot omēs, maket okhoyvnts. Monkv ēyvkerricet omvs, kicen takkakvtēs.

Mont yomocken momēn kicen takkaken ohhvyatken, mvn nake momēt oman okhoyvtētok: Hoktvke tat puhitake vlahokēpvnts, makvtēs, mahokvnts. Mont hompetv nake momēn hecvkvrē onkot ometo 'stomis, hompetv tat erocepēt 'svlahokēpet omēpekv, Punhompaks! maket omaket... Hoktvke tat mvn enheckv tat puhitaket omēpē hērēt omet omēpen, vsv hvmkat tat em punayet mont enhompet omēpen... Efv-vcule hvmket aatet vlaket cvcefokkicen, afolotkvyan, Mv hoktvke welakat cehitake tokot oman onkv em onvyvs. Mont enhompēsko tạyusēt os, maket omen... Momēn maket onkv, Enhompetskekan hērēs kicit omvyis, mvn hoktē enheckv tat ehiwv enheckvt omēpet onkv, Mvt cvhiwvt omēpan okaks, komēpet onkv enhompet... Mon em punayet estakliket 'sohyafken... Yomocken hompetv hayat tayē hēren cvfencvkē hērēt takwelaket omen... Mv efv-vculet okat, Mv hoktē cēme cehiwv omē ēyomicē tak-arat— totkv vhētkē eto estakwakkan astak-ehset, yētafolkof, 'sem aksekēyvs. Momof estomēt on okeyat, mvn kerretskvrēs.

Efvt cvkicat omēcicēn, eto vhētkat astak-ehsit, em akrēfkvyan, culv-hoktvlwvt omēpvtet kvohiket vyēpvntvs.

Momen vsv hvmkateu matapomēcekvs, kicet, mv efv-vcule tat maket ont, Em onvyvs, maken, em onayēto 'stomis, estofvn momēceko tat: Cvhiwvt vm vlaket os, komē hērēt omet... Momusen wakketv ohren, lomhet omeyan, vsv tat Mvt cvhiwvts, komē hērēt omēpekv ēpolehcet vccetv 'tem vchoyehpet wakhoket ont omis... Nake tayekot os, komikv,

Two men went hunting. And going about, they made camp and settled in. Long ago when hunters were out, they'd say, One should not think back on one's home. But now one of the hunters was homesick... No. It was said you are not to go about like that. So think about yourself, [the other] told [him] as they sat.

Then darkness came and they settled in for the night, and they have said such things happen then: Two women—it was our wives—came, he said, it was said. And even though food and the like were nowhere to be found, [the two women] had brought food, and said, Eat with us!... The women looked just like our wives, and one [hunter] talked with [his wife] and ate with her... An old dog came over and poked me, and when I turned around, said, Tell [the other man] those women that are here are not your wives. One should not eat with them, he said... And as he said that, I told [the other hunter], It is good you do not eat with them, but the woman's appearance was so like his wife's that he thought, That is my wife, and ate with her... So it was that he talked with her and sat until evening... It was getting dark and the cooks were actively going back and forth... The old dog said, That woman going around pretending to be your wife—take that piece of burning wood, and when she turns her back, gouge her with it. Then you will know everything we told you.

Because the dog had told me to, I picked up a piece of burning wood, and when I poked her, it was an old female fox who took off moaning.

Now tell the other to do the same, the old dog said, Tell him, he said, but even though I told him, he couldn't do it: My wife has come to me, he thought... Then it was time for bed, and as we were lying there, the other still thought, It's my wife, and so snuggled up to her and they lay beneath the same blanket... Something is wrong, I thought, I won't sleep, I thought,

Vneu cvnocekarēs, komit takwakkvyisan estomusē cvnocē omat, entis elēcepvtēt papet kvpotkicēpvcoken, vcvhonēcet wakkin... Efv-vcule hvtvm aatet vlaket yvn waswaket okat, Vhericēt alihket vyvs. Mon vnet ecepakarēs. Monkv em etetakvs, cvkican vtēkusen vhericēt ahuyirit, eccv raesehpet momusen em ahtin momusen vthoyēn okat, Mv este hvmkē isenloken omat, 'secepvyvranet omen okvyis maket, mv efv-vcule tat vm onayen vthoyeyvntvs, makesasvtēs, mahokvnts.

Mon efv erem ētv efv-mvnettvlke tat em punayvntvs, makesasvtēs. Mont em punayet okat, Hiyomat pupucase tat estomusen em vnicvranēn omat, em vniceyvrēs. Monkv este-honvntake omēt em vniceyvrēs. Momis cvfencakan enhopohyit 'cetotvranvkit omis. Monkv homvn vpefatiket ehketv hēran enhopoyaks. Mon mvt hēcken omat, mvn heyv pupucase tat ehkehpet ohmen pomet naket aret omen omat, 'tepoyeyvrēs, maket emvnettvlke tayen em punayvntvs, makesasvtēs. Mont lētkuset vyvs, maken, lētkusit ayin vpēyeyisan, momvranen okehpvten, tat vyetvn komvcoke ont omen... Estekene-rakkot ahakēpvcokvnts, makvtēs. Momen vpēyēn, yvwolicet vyēpvcoken... Momusen mv efv homv vpefatkat hvmket ralētket, 'yepunrapat, Ehketv punhēcket omis os. Mon mv tylkus, maket omen, Momis yi hakepusēt omēpis, maket omen... Momusen Vlecvs! cvkicaken... Momusen Letkvs! makit ayin vpēyeyat, vpēyēt eto-hvoket rakkēt wakket omen ohkvtēt on mvn erorihcēn, momusen Yvn 'cēyvs! cvkicakan vtēkusen, mv eto-hvoke tat 'ceyiyet wakkin... Momusen mv estekene-rakko tat aret okēpekv, vlahkvcoket mv eto-hvoke pikvyat ēyohhuerat, ele-kososowa 'yvropothuecēt... Mv efv-vcule avm onayet okat, Kos. Emuntvlke hēret omis os cē. Wakkvcoks, maket omen wakkin, ayen momusen estekene tat vyēpvcoken momusen okat, Mucv tat ayē hēris os, kicakvcoken pohit wakk[i]n, momusen sumkehpvcoken... Tokvs ca! Aossvs! makaken aohsvyan, mv tat 'tepoyusē hayet omēpen... Efv tat ennokkicē ont os komvkateu sasen... Hvtvm ennokkicis 'svheremahē-

and lay there, but slept for a little while... She had already killed him and was chomping noisily when I awoke and lay there... The old dog came over again and whispered, Get up carefully and go. I'll be with you. So get ready, he said to me, and right away I stood up carefully, got a gun, and came, and we both came, and he said, When she had eaten up the other person, you were going to be next, that's what I meant, the old dog told me as we came together, someone said, it was said.

And [the old dog] talked with other dogs, young dogs, someone said. And talking with them, he said, Now we're going to help our master as much as we can. So we'll help him like young men. I'll select lively ones and send you all. So run ahead and look for a good hiding place. When you find it, our owner will hide there, and we'll fight whatever is there, he said, addressing the much younger ones, someone said. Now go at a slow run, he said, and I went at a slow run and as we went, what he said would happen, happened, and it seemed he really wanted to go... A big owl is hooting in the distance, he said. And we kept going, and as it grew near, he went on... Then one of the dogs who had run ahead came back, and as he met us, [said,] We've found a hiding place. That is all, he said, But there may be something calling, he said... Then they told me, Hurry! Then I said, Run! and went, and as we all went, we kept going to where there was a big hollow log that they had meant, and upon arriving there, they told me, Get in here! and right away I got in the hollow log and lay down... The big owl was out there and came to the hollow log I was in, and as he stood on it, his claws were coming through... The old dog told me, No. He is getting tired. He is sitting, he said, and I lay there, and time went on and it seemed the big owl was leaving... Now he's really gone, I heard them say as I lay there, and it seemed he had disappeared... Now! Come out! they said, and when I came out, they were really fighting... The dogs seem hurt, some thought... Again some were hurt, though not cusekateu sasen fullet omehpvtē on... Yossin momusen mv efv-vcule tat em punayet okēpvnkekv, hvtvm em punayet okat, Vpeyatskē tayehaks? kicet oman, Vpēyeyē tis os kicakvntvs, makesasvtēs.

Mont eraweyat fullēt eryiceyvntvs. Moman hoktvke mv puhvpo erorhoyē hēceyvtē estvn vhoyesekot kakēt oman omvten, aret vne tȷlkuset rvlakvyvntvs, maket onayesasvtēs maket onahoyvnts.

Monkv fakvn arvken omat, est' encuko eravkerricē ahrēskos mahokat, fvccv-mahhet omvts, makesasvtēs, mahokvnts cē.

seriously... I came out, and as the old dog had talked with them before, he talked with them again, saying, Can you go? We will go, they said, some-one said.

And we came from there and returned. Now the two women we had seen come to our camp had not gone anywhere and were still there, and I went and returned by myself, someone has told, it was told.

So when you go hunting, do not think back on home, they used to say, and that is very true, someone said, it was said.

5

The stork father

A woman won't reveal the father of her beautiful baby. Her relatives have all the creatures ask the child to call them father, but the child ignores them. Then Stork arrives with a little fish and the child cries, "Father! Father!"

The woman's relatives try to find the father so the child will have a better standing in the community, but the joke is that it's the fish that wins the child's affection, and Stork is nothing special. In Creek, the image of the little fish skewered on a stick is comical.

Hoktē-mvnette hvmket hopuewvn ocvtēs, erke fvccekon. Mont omatet esliket omen em pohet, Estit erket on omat onvyvs, kihocēto 'stomis onvyeko tạyusēt omvtēs.

Momen mv hoktē ena-hvmkvlket fullēt omvtēs. Mont omet mvt vkerrickvn hayakvtēs. Mont okakatet, Momēt esliket estonhkotok... Estit mv estuce erket on omat esvpvkesasē tayet omētan onkv; erken enhopoyvkēts, mahket ennvkaftvtēs. Mont nvkaftet vpokvtēs, mv hoktēn ehesvrēn komaket.

Mont omen mv estuce hẹrusēt omet, yvkapusē hakepēt ont mont pu-nvkvo kerrepē hakēt arvtēs. Mon naket komvkat omỵlkvt nvkaftvtēs.

Mont mv estucen Sulet oh-ayet, Cvrkē! cvkicvs, maket arvtēs. Momis estos komēpekot ahkopvnētt vrẹpvtēs. Mont oman nake erem ētv omvlket omhoyan Akcvohkot svsekot omisat rvrucen espvkvfkusēn eshvlvtēt eroren... Mvt sekot omisat vlaks, kihocen... Atet vlakan mv estuce hecekot omisat, hēcan vtẹkuset, Cvrkē! Cvrkē! Cvrkē! kihcet ohletiket mv rvruce resem esēpvtēs.

Mohmen mv ennakvlke erke kerretv eyacakvtē, Mv este onkat omvttis! mahket enhomecēt vwahēpvtēs, mahokvnts.

A young woman gave birth to a child whose father was unknown. So she lived alone [with the child], and was asked [about that]: Tell who the father is, they'd say, but she wouldn't tell.

Now the woman had relatives. And they had an idea. And they said, She can't do well living like that... Whoever the father of the child is should marry her; let's look for his father, they said, and held a meeting. And they met, wanting the woman to have a husband.

Now the child was very beautiful and had begun to walk, and had learned to talk, as well. So all kinds of creatures had gathered.

Now Buzzard went up to the child: Call me Father! he said. But the child paid no attention and kept on playing. Now all the others were there except Stork, who had been absent and arrived carrying a little fish skewered on a stick... He wasn't even here before and now here he comes, they said... As he arrived the child didn't see him, but as soon as he saw him, he ran up to him, cried, Father! Father! Father! and took the little fish.

Then those relatives who had wanted to find out who the father was said, [That stork] doesn't even look like anyone special! and dismissed the meeting in anger, it was said.

6

Rabbit steals fire

There is no fire on this island, so a meeting is called. After everyone else refuses, Rabbit is put in charge of getting fire from overseas. He runs across the water and comes to a house, saying he's a dance leader. He begins to lead a dance, smears tar on his hands and head, puts a live coal on his head, and returns with the fire (cf. Swanton 1929, Creek stories 43, 44).

Dance leaders sometimes make alternating up-and-down motions with their arms as they dance, turning periodically to face the fire. In exaggerating that movement, Rabbit is able to reach down and snatch the fire. The island referred to in this well-known story may be North America (see also story 13).

Cufet totkv heckuecet omvtēs, mahokvnts. Yv otē totkv sekot omen, nvkaftet estit totkv heckuecē tayat maket vpoket omhoyen... Cufet okat, Vnet heckuecvyēs, makvtēs. Momis em enhonrekot omet: Estit omē tayat mvn omē tas, kihocē 'stomis, Vcomepekot os, makvkephoyē-vlket ont oman... Vnet omarēs, Cufet makętt omen... Momusen, Momēcē tayat okēs, kihocvtēs.

Moman totkvt tvpalv-rakkon ocepēt omvtēs. Mont omen mv totkvn eyacet okhoyekv, momusen wiketv hahoyvtēs.

Mvn okēpekv, vyēpvtēs. Mv uewv-rakko tat akletiket vyēpat, ąyet tikēpvtēs. Mont cuko likēn eroren... Este kerrēskot vlaket os, kihocet omet... Likepvs, kihocen, liket omen, estvmvn vtēt omat em pohohen... Min vtvyēt mi tat afvcketv ǫmusis sąseseko hakepēt ont omen; estvn afvcketv omusis ocephoyusis ocen omat, estehēcē vretv cvmvlostē hęrēt omēpan omen... Yvmv tat estvn afvcketv svsēpis omēs komvken, momusen arit omis, maket omen... Kos. Mon omat, opvnkvn vpeyvranet vpoket omēkv, vpeyvkvrēs, pum etetakof, kihocen likvtēs. Mont em pohaket, Opvnkv 'senhomahtv tis omētskis omēs? kicaken... Mvn ę vm maketvt omēs! maket omen... Mv este mv oman pumvlostē hęrēt omētok... Mon omat, pum etetaket onkv vpeyvkēs, kihocet ohmen, est vcakkayvtēs.

Mon fullet eroricet omen, opvnkv tat tayē hęren opanet vpoket omhoyen, eralikvtēs. Momen mv ēyvpvyē resoricat okaket: Momēn este kerrēskot aret omat, Eshomahtvt omēpvyēs, makēpet vrēpet omēpisan omatskes, kicaken... Momusen em pohvtohyen, momusen atakhvtvpiket momusen vlicehcet tayē hęren yvhiket... Mvn vnkomatskēt omis, maket yvhiket onkv, vhere-mahe ont takliket omen... Omylkuset em vnicvkēs, hvm-makof, kicet, em vcahnet omhoyen... Mv etvlwv vtēhkat omylkuse ont

It's said that Rabbit acquired fire. This island had no fire, so there was a meeting to discuss who would be able to get fire... Rabbit said, I can get it. But they didn't believe in him: Someone more able should be the one, they said, yet each one said, I'm not able to do it... I'll do it, Rabbit kept saying... So finally they said, Maybe he can do it.

During this time, there was fire overseas. And since fire was badly needed [here], [Rabbit] was put in charge.

Because he meant what he'd said, he started off. He ran and ran across the ocean until he had crossed it. Then he came to a house... Someone we do not know has arrived, they said... Have a seat, they said, and as he sat, they asked him where he was from... I come from afar where there is no happiness; I thought there may be some place where people have a little happiness... I enjoy traveling and meeting people in different places, and I thought there may be happiness here somewhere, so that's why I'm here, he said... You don't say. Well, then, we're going to a dance, so we'll all go when we get ready, they told him. Then they asked him, Might you be a dance leader? Oh, that's my specialty! he said... That's the kind of person we love, they said... Well, we're ready, so let's go, they said, and he went with them.

They arrived, and as the dance was in full swing, he sat nearby. And the people who had brought him along said: We have a stranger here who says, I'm a leader; maybe he would lead, they said... Then he was invited, and he got down by the fire and started singing loudly... This is what you want of me, he said, singing, really exaggerating as he danced... Let's all help him as he leads, they said, encouraging him... Almost all the tribal towns helped him as he led, and he thought, This is what I wanted, and em vnihocen estakliket omen, Tayepvtēs, kont oh-vrakkuehocē hḕre-mahen... Opanet on omis, Totkvn eyacet aret okan kerrekot omhoyen... 'Sem vhopayat, totkv tis estak-ēsē hayet omen... Ayen mvn okekv enke colokcowvn vlofēt omat, totkv tak-ehset, hvtvm ekv-nvrkvpvn matv-pomēn ohlofēt omvtet, torvwvn 'kohlihcet momusen 'senletiken... Assēcet, Totkvn espunlētket os, kicet omhoyis cakhokekon rastikvtēs.

Mvt totkv heckuecvtēt omistvnts, mahokvnts cē.

was greatly honored... Although he was dancing, his mission was to get the fire, but they didn't know this... He made motions, pretending to pick up the fire... Time passed, and as he intended, he smeared tar on his hands, picked up the fire, and having more tar smeared on the middle of his head, put a live coal on his head and started running... They chased him, saying, He's running away with our fire, but they didn't catch him and he crossed back over.

Thus he obtained fire, it was said.

7

Turtle is beaten by three mothers

Turtle asks some baby skunks what clan they are. When they tell him they are Skunk clan, he makes them cry by saying he skunked around with their mother. Then he makes some baby raccoons cry by saying he cooned around with their mother. Finally, he makes some baby opossums cry by saying he possumed around with their mother. Mother Skunk finds her children crying and they tell her what happened. She becomes furious and finds Raccoon, whose children say the same thing. Both go to Opossum, who has had the same experience. They find Turtle and beat him to a pulp. He sings a song and his shell is patched together.

This story is often told without the sexual content, but Turtle's lechery is crucial to the story. As in story 27, it's his lewd comments that lead to his broken shell. A similar version of the story is recorded in Yuchi (Wagner 1931:43–46).

Lucvt arvtēs. Mont omet aret oman, konucvlket vpokēt omen roret em pohet okat: Cecke nakvlke toyēs, makētvnka? kicen... Konovlke toyēs, makētvnks, kicaken... Moman vsin erayvtēton, 'sem vkonokuecvyisan ahyen atit omis, kihcet, vyēpen hvkihhoket vpokvtēs.

Mont hvtvm ayan, hvtvm Wotkucvlket vpoken erem orvtēs. Mont mvo em pohvtēs. Mont okat, Cecke nakvlke toyēs, makētvnka? kicen... Wotkvlke toyēs, makētvnks, kicaken... Moman omēs. Vsin erayvtēton, 'sem vwotwuecvyisat atit omis, mvo kihcet, vyēpen mvo hvkihhoket vpokvtēs.

Momen hvtvm hoyahnet ayat, hvtvm sukhv-hatkucvlket vpoken hvtvm erem orvtēs. Mont mvo em pohet okat: Naket pum vliketvts, cecke makētvnka? kicen... Sukhv-hatkvlke toyēs, makētvn[k]s, kicaken... Okat, Moman omēs. Vsin erayvtēton, 'sem vhathicvyisan, ahyen atit omis, kicen, mvo hvkihhoket vpoken...

Momusen Kono tạwvt ervlaket oman, mv echustake momēn hvkihhoket vpoken... Yehēcet omet, Naket estomen hvkihhokatskehaks? kicen... Momēn Lucvt vlaket omat, Cecke nakvlke toyēs, makētvnka? maket vpohet omen... Konovlke toyēs, makēt omētvnks, kiceyan, Moman omēs. Vsin erayvtēton, 'sem vkonokuecvyisan, ahyen atit omis, maket vlahket yvyēpet ohman, hvkihhoket okēs, kicaken... Momusen cvpvkiket, ayat fvccvn ayan, hvtvm wotkucvlket vpoken, eckeu liken ont oman, mvo hvkihhoken omen... Naket estomen puetake hvkihhoka? kicet erem pohen... Moman Lucvt maket aret os, maket omaket mvn hvkihhoket okēs, maket vpoken... Rvlahkvyatet likit omis, kicen... Mon omat, mvn

There once was a turtle. And he went to the home of a family of baby skunks and asked them: Did your mother say what clan we are? She used to say we're Skunk clan, they said... It must be, [he said,] she was walking over there, and I skunked around with her, and then she went on her way and I came this way, he said, and as he left, they sat and cried.*

As he was walking along he came upon some little raccoons. And he asked them, too. Did your mother say what clan we are? he asked... She used to say we're Raccoon clan, they said... It must be so. She was walking over there, and I cooned around with her and came this way, he said to them, too, and as he left, they, too, sat and cried.

After going by there, again he came to where some little opossums lived. And he asked them, too: Did your mother say what our clan is? She used to say we're Opossum clan, they said... It must be so, he said. She was walking over there, and after I possumed around with her, she went on her way and I came this way, he said, and they, too, sat and cried...

After a while [Mother] Skunk returned and found her children crying like that... Coming up and seeing them, she asked, Why are you crying? Turtle came by, [they said,] and asked, Did your mother say what clan we are? She used to say we're Skunk clan, we said, and he said, It must be so. She was walking over there, and after I skunked around with her, she went on her way and I came this way, he said and left, and that's why we are crying, they said... She became furious, and going in the direction he went, she came upon some little raccoons with their mother, and they, too, were crying... Why are the babies crying? she asked... Well, Turtle is going around saying things and we are crying, they told me... I just

* This story contains verbs that were created to play off the words for skunk, raccoon, and opossum in Creek.

assēcit arit omis, mvn kicof, Mon omat, vneu cecakkvyarēs, kihcen vhoyvtēs.

Mont vhoyat, hvtvm sukhv-hatkucvlket vpokēt omen erorhoyen, mvo hvkihhoket vpoken... Eckeu ralaket mvo esliken erorhoyet em pohaket okat, Naket estomen hvkihhokēs makaken esliket ontskehaks? kicaken... Momēn Lucvt vlaket omat, Cecke nakvlke toyēs makēt omētvnka? maken, Sukhv-hatkvlke toyēs, makēt omētanks, kiceyan... Moman omēs. Vsin erayvtēton, 'sem vhathicvyisan, ahyen atit omis, maket vlahket yvyēpet ohman, mvn hvkihhoket okēs, makaket omen eslikit omis, kicet em onahyen... Pomeu matvpomēn pukicet aret atet omvcoken, puetake matvpomēn hvkihhoket vpoken ohmvten arit atvyat yi Wotkon iem vlakvyan, mvo matvpomēn taklikvthaken, momusen hvtvm mvn yetepahkēt, mv este lucv hopoyet vthọyēt yvn vlahoket omēs. Monkv estvn aren omat hecetvn kont hopoyet omēs, kicet omaken... Mon omat, vneu vyarēs, Sukhvo mahken, momusen vpēyvtēs.

Mont fullet mv lucv tat rehcakkakvtēs. Eton rvwvlvpkeko tayet vliken cvkiket... Mvn kont fullet okekv, momusen erem pohaket omis, enhome-cvkēt fullet okekv, momusen nvfiket, nạfket, nạfket, nạfket cetạkkusēn hahyet ervwēpvtēs.

Momēn likvtēs. Mv lucv elekon wiket omhoyen likvtēs. Mont okatet ē-em posket liket okat yvhikvtēs. Momat mv nafkē wokochoyat etelikvrē vrahkvn omvtēs. Mont okat,

> Cvte-lih-lih,
> Cvte-lih-lih,

returned and found them crying, she said... Well, that's who I'm chasing after, [Skunk said,] and as she said this, [Mother Raccoon] said, Well, then, I'll go with you, and they started out.

And as they went they came to where the little opossums lived, and they were crying, too... Their mother was there with them, and they asked, Why do they say they're crying? Turtle came and asked them, Did your mother say what clan we are? and the little opossums told him, She used to say we're Opossum clan... It must be so, [he said], She was walking over there, and after I possumed around with her, she went on her way and I came this way, he told us and left, and that is why we're crying, they told me... That is the very same thing he said about us as he went about, and I returned to find my children crying so I went to Raccoon's and she had had the same thing happen to her, and we got together, and we've come looking for that turtle. And wherever he is we want to find him, they said... Well, then, I'll go, too, Opossum said, and they started out.

And they caught up with the turtle. He was sitting there unable to cross a log when they caught up with him... They meant business, so they asked him about it, but they were so angry at him that they beat him and kept beating him and kept beating him and kept beating him until he was just pulp and came home.

He sat there like that. They left him alive and he sat there. As he sat fasting for himself, he sang. [The fasting and song] were for the shattered pieces of his shell to come back together. And he sang,

> I come-come together,
> I come-come together,

Cvte-sokoso,
Cvte-lih-lih,
Cvte-sokoso,

maket liket ayen, momusen mvn okekv eteliket mont etelokpet omvtēs.

Monkv mvn nafket omhoyvtēs. Momen mvt omēs. Lucv hēcatskat, cetakkvtē omēt omēs.

Monkv mvt Kono mont Wotko momet Sukhv-hatkv esyomat nvfkakvtēt omēs, maket onahoyēt omvnts. Monkv Lucv tat ehvrpe encetakkēto 'stomis elekot omēs, maket okhoyvnts, mahokvnts cē.

I shake-shake together,
I come-come together,
I shake-shake together,

and as he sat, gradually as he sang, [the shell pieces] came back together and stuck together.

So he was badly beaten. And that's how it is. When you see a turtle, [the shell] looks like it's been smashed into pieces.

So it was Skunk and Raccoon and Opossum who beat him, it's been told. So even though Turtle's shell is crushed, he doesn't die, it's been said.

8

Rabbit rides Wolf

To impress a young woman, Rabbit gets Wolf to act as his horse. Wolf is abused, is attacked by the woman's dogs, and escapes. After a long time, Wolf comes upon Rabbit again and captures him. Rabbit tells him about a dead horse nearby, a horse that is actually just sleeping. Rabbit ties the horse's tail around Wolf's neck and shouts for him to eat. Wolf bites down and the horse takes off with him (cf. Swanton 1929, Creek stories 72–74).

Rabbit shows his complete mastery of the more powerful wolf by tricking him twice in this story.

Cufet arvten, hvtvm Yvhvt hvtvm aret omen, 'tefaccvtēs. Mohmen Cufet okat, Yvhvn oket, Ecohlikin welakvkēs, kicvtēs.

Moman Cufe tat hoktē mvnetten licephoyēt ont omen mvn estem eyacet aret omvtēs. Mont ont mvn esvyetvn eyacet okvtēs. Yvhvn 'mvkerrēt okan mv yvhv tat kērresekatēs.

Mont mv cufe tat mvn okekv, Ecohlikvranis kicet omen, 'mvkvsamekv momusen Cufe tat Yvhvn ohlihket esayvtēs. Mv hoktē likan 'sayet 'saret okat Escefketvn 'svcakcvhēcin omvkēs kicen... Momepekvs, Yvhv tat makvtēs. Mon mvn okekv, Cufe tat ahvtvpiket oklvfonvn hopoyehpet, mvn ele-ceskvn vlumhicet ohmet, momusen, Tokvs! Vm etetakētt os kihcet ohlihken, hvtvm 'sayvtēs.

Mont 'sayofvn Cufet oket, Vhoyvken, mv hoktē eyacē likan okvtēs, mv cuko ervwolicēn omat, momusen 'co-rakko cvfeknē arvnto omēt, vtakhataket lētkuset ontsken erorhoyvkvrēs, mv cukon, kicvtēs.

Momen mvn okekv, momusen mv cuko vhēckan eresoren momusen Cufe tat escefketv mv yvhv tat momusen 'sem vcēfken, mvn momet omvranat mvhayēt omēpekv kerrētatēs, Yvhv tat. Monkv momusen Yvhv tat 'sem vcefhoken lētkuset, vtakhatakuset aren, mv cuko okat eresorvtēs. Mont roret omen, Likepvs cē! mv hoktē eyahocat ecket kicvtēs. Momen mvn komēpatet aret oman okhoyekv, momusen ahvtvpiket likvtēs.

Mont mv yvhv tat fettvtēken etot takcakhēt ont omen mvn ervwvnayet takhuericvtēs. Mon Cufe tat est etem punayat cuko ofv min rataklikvtēs. Momen mv yvhv tat takhuervtēs, vwvnvkēt. Moman efvn ohocēt omvtēs.

As Rabbit was going about, Wolf, too, was about, and they met. Then Rabbit said to Wolf, Let me sit on you and we can go about.

Now Rabbit knew about a young lady living [with her parents] whom he wanted very much. And that was the reason he wanted to get Wolf to take him there. Wolf didn't know he was being tricked.

Then, determined, the rabbit said, I'm going to get up on you, and he agreed, so Rabbit got up on Wolf's back and started out. He was going to where the girl lived, and said to him, Let me put on some spurs... Very well, Wolf said. He was serious, so Rabbit got down and gathered cockle-burrs, stuck them to his heels, and then said, There! I'm ready, and got back up on him and started out once more.

And as [Wolf] was taking him, Rabbit said, As we go, meaning where the girl he wanted lived, when we get near that house, you must immediately act like a really lively horse, prancing sideways and galloping as we arrive at the house, he said.

Then just as he said, when they were within sight of the house, Rabbit immediately used the spurs on the wolf and poked him, and as he had been instructed, Wolf knew what to do. So as the spurs were jabbing him, he began to trot, and sometimes prancing sideways, he brought [Rabbit] to the house he had told him about. Arriving there, the mother of the girl he wanted said, Have a seat! And this was exactly what [Rabbit] wanted them to say, so he immediately climbed off and sat down.

There was a tree on the edge of the yard, and there the wolf stood where [Rabbit] had tied him. Now Rabbit sat in the house talking to the people. And the wolf was standing outside tied up. Now these people had dogs.

Moman Cufe tat este 'tem punvyēpat taklikēpen... Vyēpen hofonē haken hvtvm hompetvn enkvlephoyen hompēpet Cufe tat cuko ofvn likēpvcoken, Yvhv tat takhuervtēs.

Momen hompvtē wihohkvcoken pvlaknv tat momusen okkoset omatet pvlaknv okkoskvn efvn em vcanet omat, mv yvhv takhuerat tempen erem vcvnhoyet omen... Mv efvt pvlaknv-okkoskvn ēskatet 'setepoyat, mv yvhv min vcvpokset esaken... Momusen Cufe tat lētket yosset omis, mv yvhv tat es wvnakvn tahcet letkēpvtēs. Mohmen Yvhv tat vyepemahvtēs. Momen Cufe tat yopvn ayvtēs.

Mont omis Cufe mont Yvhv etehecekon hofonēn welakvtēs. Mont omvtētan vyēpen hofonē haken Yvhv tat arvtēs. Mont aret omaten, Cufe tat toskōnkot liken eshēcvtēs.

Mont omet okat, Vnhessē! Naket estoman mōmvtēken vm vkērret ometskvt ton omat kerretv kont arvyēt ont os. Hiyomat on omat cesvlafket os, kicvtēs.

Mon Cufe tat likvtēs. Naken maketv kerreko ont omis mv tempe hakvranan cerakkot nocēt wakken hēcet omvtēs. Mon mvn oket, Vsin corakkot elepvtēt wakkēt omis. Monkv mvn ercem onahyin mvn vc vyopuskēn hompetskēs, kicvtēs. Mon omat, mvo momēs kihcet mv cufe nake ēlv wakkat 'svyvranat 'mvkvsamvtēs.

Mohmen mv hvte Yvhv Cufe eshēcē svlvfkuecof, mv cufe elehcet lokvranat tvlket oken mvn Cufe tat kērret ont, mvn cerakko nocē wakkan hēcet liket omof ohmen mvn iem onahyet efekhayvtēs.* Momusen mvn

* The meaning of *efekhayvtēs* is uncertain, but looks like *efēke* 'his heart' and *hayvtēs* 'he made'.

And Rabbit continued to sit [in the house] and talk... Time passed and after a long time, they shared a meal with him and Rabbit stayed in the house while Wolf stood outside.

Then the meal was over and the dishes were being washed, and the dishwater was poured for the dogs, close to where the wolf stood... The dogs were drinking the dishwater and started fighting over it, and then they surrounded the wolf and attacked him... Immediately Rabbit came out running, but the wolf had broken the rope and run away. So Wolf got away. And Rabbit left later.

So it was that Rabbit and Wolf didn't see each other for a long time. After this, a long time passed and Wolf was going about. While he was going about, he found Rabbit sitting around inattentively.

So [Wolf] said, My Friend! I've been wanting to know why you played such a big trick on me. As of now you're a prisoner, he said.

Rabbit just sat there. He didn't know what to say, but close by he'd seen a horse sleeping. And he said, Over there lies a dead horse. So I'll go and show you, and you can eat it instead of me, he said. Well, then, let it be so, [Wolf] said, and the rabbit agreed to take him to the carcass.

At the time that Wolf found Rabbit and took him prisoner, Rabbit had known that [Wolf] was going to kill him and eat him, and having just seen the sleeping horse lying there, he told him about it. Then as he had okekv ēyvpahyet 'sayvtēs. Mont mv corakko wakkat res orvtēs. Mont okat, Ehvcen hērren cenokwvn cem vcokcohrin, Tokvs! makvyof, momusen pvpetskvrēs kicen mvo em vkvsamvtēs.

Momen momusen mvn okekv ehvce-essen mv yvhv nokwvn 'sem vwv-nayet yekcēn estohmet recvpeko tayēn 'sem vwvnahyet, momusen Tokvs! makin omat, momusen pvpepetskvrēs. Orēn nake herēn cem etetakuecit omis. Monkv ētusēn vyehpit Hokvs! makarēs kihcet, momusen ētusēn vkuekehpet, Hokvs! kihcen momusen em ak-vkiken nocepēt wakket oman okehpvten... Akkan, momusen mv corakko tat feksumecihcen astasiket es lētken... Cufet okat, Vnhessē! Ceyvllvs! kicen... Yvhvt okat, Kot estohmit ceyvllvyē tayen kērret momēn cvkicet oketskehaks? maket, Vtarken es letecihcet... Cufe tat mvn lvkiset ēhesayēcehpet momusen vyēpvtēs, mahokvnts cē.

said, he took him. And they arrived where the horse lay. And he said, Let me wrap its tail securely around your neck, and when I say Now! you start eating it, he said, and [Wolf] agreed.

So then as he said, he took the hair of the tail and wrapped it around the wolf's neck tightly, and he tied it so that there was no way he could get it loose, and then he said, When I say Now! you'll eat. I've prepared something very good for you. So I'll go a little distance, and say Now, he said, and then he moved a short distance, and as soon as he said Now! Wolf bit into [the horse's] rear end, though he was only sleeping... As soon as he bit him, he startled the horse, and he jumped up and started running [off with him]... Rabbit yelled, My Friend! Pull hard! And Wolf said, Are you telling me you know a way I can pull hard enough? Rabbit ran [the horse] off with him hanging on... Rabbit lied and saved himself, and then went away, they used to say.

9

Turtle races Wolf

Turtle invites Wolf to a race through four ravines. Turtle says he'll wear a white feather, and then secretly places four other turtles with white feathers in each ravine. When the race begins, Wolf discovers the turtle is always ahead of him and is defeated (cf. Swanton 1929, Creek story 59).

Felix Gouge, who also tells this story, states that the white feather used here and in story 3 is a peaceful feather. The story is sometimes told with Deer or Rabbit in place of Wolf.

Lucvt Yvhvn 'tem arvtēs mahokvnts. Mont omen Lucvt okat, 'Tem vrēpvkēs, Yvhv kicvtēs. Momen Yvhvt okat, Kos! Vm orihcetskekos kicvtēs. Momen Lucvt okat, Momis vnet okēpikv... 'Tentokorikēn estin emmuntvlken omat kērrvkēs kicet omen... Mon omat momētis okis. Cēmet okētskis okikv kihcet, Yvhv tat em vkvsamvtēs.

Momen momusen mvn okēpekv, Lucv tat ēyvhoporrenkvtēs. Moman mv 'tem vrvranat pvne ostan esti tat eroren omat mvt vkoslat omvrēs maketvn etem vkvsamet omvtēs. Momen Lucvt okat, Tafv hvtkucen 'kvcakhēcit omarēs makvtēs. Mvt esvm ēkērkvt omvrēs kicvtēs. Mont okēpekv, Lucv tat tafv hvtkuce osten hopoyēpvtēs. Mont hvtvm lucv osten hopoyēpvtēs. Mont mv lucv ostat omilkvn tafv hvtkuce 'kohcakcvhēcepicvtēs. Momet ēkvnv kērken 'tem vrvranet okēpekv, mv lucv tat mv pvne ostat omvlkvn 'setetayēcvtēs. Pvne hvmken tvyiket, hvtvm pvne hvmkan erahecakat, hēcvkē tayen licet mv pvne ostat omvlkvn 'setetayēn, lucv vpoyēpvtēs. Hvte mv nettv oreko monken omvtēs. Momis mv yvhv tat momēn mv lucv vhoporrenkat kērresekatēs. Monkv mv lucv hvmkusēn 'tem vrvranit omis komat tilkuset vrēpvtēs.

Momen ayen mv nettv okakvtē cakkēt omen, Yvhv tat ayvtēs. Mont eroran, Lucv tat erorepēt liken erorvtēs. mont mv lucv tat enhomvn em etetakētt omvtētok. Vm etetakepēt os, Lucv tat maket, tafv hvtkuce 'kvcakhēcēpvntut likvtēs. Momen Yvhvo, Vm etetakētut os kicet omen... Hokvs! makin omat, momusen ayvyat okarēs. Monkv Hokvs! makin omat, momusen vhoyvkvrēs kicen... Momepekvs, Yvhvt kicvtēs.

Momusen em etetakahket ohmen, Hokvs! Lucv tat makvtēs. Mont lētkē hahyet matan likēpvtēs. Moman Yvhv tat, Tokvs! kihocekv hēre mahen ayat, pvne hvmken tiket ervhēcan, hvtvm pvne hvmkan erossepvrąnuset pihket avliken hehcet... Momusen Yvhv tat omvlkucvn ayat, hvtvm pvne

Turtle and Wolf had a race, it's been said. Now Turtle said to Wolf, Let's race. Then Wolf said, No! You can't keep up with me. Then Turtle said, But I want to... Let's run and find out who will be defeated, he said... Well, all right, then. We will since you're the one who wants to, Wolf said in agreement.

Then, as [Wolf] agreed, Turtle began to lay serious plans for himself. The first racer to get to the fourth ravine will be the winner, they agreed. Then Turtle said, I'll wear a white feather on my head. That will be my sign, he said. And as he said, Turtle looked for four little white feathers. And then Turtle looked for four [other] turtles. And he made all four turtles put white feathers on their heads. Then because he had chosen a familiar place for the race, the turtle prepared all four ravines with a turtle in each one. He went across one ravine [to the second one], and looked back at the first, placed a turtle where it could be seen clearly [from the first ravine], and set turtles down in each of the four ravines. He did this before the day of the race. But the wolf did not know that the turtle had figured out a scheme. So he went around thinking he was racing just the one turtle.

Time passed, and the appointed day arrived, so Wolf went. So when he arrived, Turtle was already there, for the turtle was ready ahead of time. I'm ready, Turtle said, and sat fixing a white feather on his head. Then Wolf said, I'm ready, too... When I say Now! it'll mean I'm starting. So when I say Now! we will start right away, [Turtle] said... Let it be so, Wolf said to him.

As soon as they were ready, Turtle said, Now! Now [Turtle] pretended to run, but just sat in the same place. But as soon as Now! was said, Wolf took off, crossed the first ravine and looked ahead, but saw Turtle just coming out of the next ravine whooping as he climbed... Then Wolf went hvmkan tiket hvtvm ervhēcan... Mvn mont omēpētok hvtvm pvne erhvmke tat hvtvm tikētt rossepēt mvo pihkat erossēpen... Yvhv tat omvlkucvn hueret omis, pvne ostan mahket 'tem vkvsamvtētok, mv pvne ostat mv lucv tąwvt erossehpet... Yvhv letketv ēkvsvmē arvtē Lucvt hęre mahen ohhoporreniket, Lucvt Yvhvn 'montahlet, Yvhvn vlesketvn enhayatēt omēs maket onahoyvnts cē.

forward with all his strength, crossed another ravine, and looked ahead again... And as before, [Turtle] had already crossed the next ravine and was coming out, he came out whooping as he climbed... Though Wolf kept at it with all his might, they had agreed on four ravines, and from those four ravines the turtle came out first... Wolf was always arrogant about his ability to run, but Turtle planned wisely, Turtle defeated Wolf, and Wolf is still envious, it was told.

10
The young man who turned into a snake

Two young men go hunting. One discovers eggs along a riverbank and is warned not to eat them. He eats one of the eggs anyway. By morning, he has turned into a snake all the way up to his head, and he tells his friend to drag him in a circle and leave. Where he swings him, a great body of dangerous water appears. The friend brings the young man's grandmother to see him. The snake comes out and lies against his grandmother before taking her under (cf. Swanton 1929, Creek stories 23–27).

There are many versions of this legend told among Yuchis, Seminoles, Alabamas, and others (Lankford 1987:83–105; Grantham 2002:199–227). It describes the origin of ue-pucase 'water master' or estakwvnayv 'tie-snake' (see also story 3) and teaches that tragedy will strike those who fail to heed warnings. As in story 4, one man listens to his conscience and one man does not. In some versions, the snake creates a body of water, sometimes also leading to the destruction of a great town.

Hoktvlē hvmket em osuswv este-mvnette orēn ocēt likvtēs, mahokvnts. Mont omvtētan fayetvn vpēhoyen, vyetvn maken... Mometskē tis os, epuset kihcen, este hvmken 'tepahket vhoyvtēs.

Mont welaket vhoyat, welaket hvpo hayvntut... Vhoyēpet hopvyēn eror- hoyen, ehvpo hayaken fayakat welaket omaten... Mv este-mvnettat fayat arvtētat rvlaket okat: Nake echustaket owv vfopken mv tạt hervkēt kakis, maket, mv 'tepvkē welakan yem onayen... Mv hvmkat okatet, Kos! Celahyēskos. Nake herekis omēs, kicet, em vsēhvtēs.

Momen hvtvm ayat, aret rvlaket omat, Hvtvm rvrot mv hervkēt 'toke- ceskvn vtēhken hecit omis maket hvtvm yem onayen... Mvo nake herekis omēs. Celahyēskos, kicet em vsēhē monket omen welakvtēs. Mv nake hēcē makat celayekatēs.

Mon welaket omvtētan, mvn nake ocakan hecēpet vrēpet emonkvtēs. Mont mv nake pvpetvn eyacētatēs. Mont omis mv hvmkat em vsēhat omēcicēn celayekot. Vrusē hayet, Estomēt ont on omat pahpin hoyvnekvs komvtēs. Mont mv hvmkat 'monạyesekot mv nake echustake hvmken esehpet eresvtehpet, hvmken pvpēpvtēs, hvmkat kerrekon.

Mon pvpehpof, em onayvtēs. Mon mv hvmkat okat: Nake herekis omēton ọkvyvnkan papet ontskes kicet omis pvpēpekv aren takkaket omvtētan, yomuckētt omen wakhokvtēs.

Mon nochoyēpvtētan, vhonēcan, naket nak mạkē 'sem mont vhonēcvtēs. Mont vhonecēt takwakkof, kotetẹcket takwakket omacoken pohet... Mv hvmkat takwakken mv nak makē okē wakkat okatet, Alihket cvhecvs, naket cvstomet on omat, kicet omen, alihket oh-ahyet hēcan, entis nvrkvtēkat cettot hocackētt takwakket okēpen hēcvtēs.

An old lady once lived with her young grandson, they used to say. Some people were going hunting and he wanted to go... You may go, his grand- mother said, and after he joined another man, they went.

And as they went, they made camp along the way... They went far and arrived at a place where they made camp and went hunting... The young man who'd been out hunting returned, saying: There are some good- looking eggs sitting beside the water... The other hunter said, No! One must not touch them. It may be something bad, he said, and forbade him.

Then again he went, and on returning, told him, This time I saw some good fish in a stump... That too may be something bad. Do not touch them, [the other hunter] said, still forbidding him. He did not touch what he had seen and described.

And as they went about, he kept looking at those things he had seen. And he wanted to eat them. Yet because of the other's warning, he did not touch them. He was all right for a while until he thought, I'm going to eat it and see how it is. So without telling the other [hunter], he took one egg, brought it back, and ate it without the other knowing.

After he ate it, he told him. Then the other [hunter] said: I told you it may be bad but you've eaten it, and since he had already eaten it, they just sat around, and as it was dark, they went to bed.

After they fell asleep, one awoke thinking he was hearing something. As he lay there awake he heard the other lying there making squeaky sounds... The one lying there making the noises said, Get up and look at me, see what is happening to me, he said, and the other one got up and went to see, and he saw that he had already become a snake up to his stomach.

Mohmet okat, Mvn nake momis omēton okvyvnkekv, nake tayeko mahēt ecohcakket omes cē, kicvtēs. Momen okat, Momis hoyvnēpet omētis os, maket takwakken nocēpvtēs.

Momen hvyatkan yi em ena tat omylkvt cettot hakep[ē] pokēpen: ekv tylkuset vhosken hvyatkvtēs. Mont omis opunayusē monkvtēs. Mont okatet, mv 'tepakvtēn oket, Heyv hiyomē nake cvmomat cvwihket yefulkepetskvrēs. Momis hvte vyeko monket cayvpahyet, ēkvnv enrakkē 'metetayen, poloksēn escvfulotiket, ētusēn vyepetskvrēs. Momen vm ehaketsken uewvn akcēyehpin vyepvccvs. Momis mv momē cvmomē-cetskat vyeko monket roretskvrēs. Estohakēs? kontsken omat, mv ēkvnv ercvwiketskat erorvccvs, kicvtēs.

Mohmen mvn okekv, ena omylkvt cetto-capko hakē pokehpen, momusen ēyvpahyet 'sayat eto-vlkat 'sayet, mvn kicet okekv, 'sayet, eresfulotiket es poloksicat, ēkvnv lvpvtkēt omet, naket momē ocvrē tokot eto-vlkēt omvtētat, mv 'sayē resfulotkat vtēkat, uewvt estvmahē hakehpen, mv eto sasvtēto 'stomis aktultoken, naket akseko hakehpet uewv sēhoneckē estvmahet likehpen... Aret eravtēpvtet, Estomvranen okat omat rahehcit vyehpvyē tat omis, kohmet... Ayet mv uewv vtēkusan erhueren, uewv tat 'stvmahet omēpen hēcet hueren... Mv uewv aknvrkvpv mahen uewv oksētkē rakkot osiyet, sēhoneckēt ocet omis hueren... Mv este cetto hakvtē ak-vrēpet omehpvtet, mv uewv nvrkvpvn afvnken hēcet hueren, aksumiken huerē monken, hvtvm vkuekusēt hvtvm yvfvnket omis. Mvt 'tepvkeyē welakeyvtēt omētis os komet hueren... Hvtvm aksumkat uewv yvtēkvn yvfvniket omen... Mv onvpvn hueret onkv, aosiyet, estvmahet cetto-cvpko hakēt omēpekv yewakket omis... 'Punvkv tat ehosepē saset omis, 'punayusē monket omen, mv em etepvketv em punayet okat: Hi-yomat vyepvranetskehaks? kicen... Komit omvyis. Estomvranen oketskvt omat espokē cehehcit vyēpit omarēs, kohmit atit omis, kicen... Momētt

Then he said, I tried to tell you that it might be bad, and now something really bad has caught up with you, he said. It has come to pass, [the snake-man] lay on the floor while [the other hunter] went to sleep.

And in the morning his whole body had turned into a snake: only his head was still [human] when morning came. He could still talk a little, though. And he told his partner, Since this thing has happened to me, you must leave me and go back. But before going, take me to a roomy spot, take me around in a circle, and move to another area. And wait for me until I go into the water, then leave. But before you leave, you must come back. If you want to know how I am, you can come to the place where you left me, he said.

Then the unavoidable happened as his whole body became a long snake, and then [the other] took him into the woods, as he had been instructed, and where he dragged him around in a circle in the woods, it didn't appear there could be anything but forest, wherever he had taken him and dragged him around became a great body of water, and the trees and everything that had been there fell into the water and disappeared, and the great body of water became supernatural... As he started back he thought, I'll go see what he meant would happen and then I should leave... He went to the water's edge and stood, and saw that the body of water was very large... Near the middle of the water, a great trough appeared, and he stood knowing the water was dangerous... He saw it was the man who had partially turned into a snake surfacing in the middle of the water, and as he stood there watching, [the snake] went under again and came up again not far from the first place. We went around together, [the man] recalled, standing there... Again [the snake] went under and came up along the edge of the water... Because [the man] was standing above him, he came up, and having become a great, long snake, he just lay there...

os, maket hvkihket omis, momusen estonko tąyuset uewv hayehpet likēpen em punayvtēs. Em punayet okat, Cvpuse tat cvhecetv tylkusis yecvhecvrēs. ēyvpahyet resahtetsken cvhecvrēs. Momen vlahokatskat, cvpuse tat uewv onvpusan ēyohlikvrēs. Momen cēmet ētusēn liket svokvn hayēcet, 'mvyvhiketsken, vrętt vm etetaken aossarēs, kihcet... Momusen hvlvlątket mv ue-hvsē-rakko akcēyehpen, momusen mv 'tepakvtētat ervtēpvtēs.

Mont mvn okvtētok, vrępet ervlakat, ąyet mv este-mvnette cetto hakvtē epuse likan erohret em onayvtēs. Mohmen mvn okvtētok, mv hoktalat hvkįhket liken... Momusen estvmvtut on omat hecvranvyat tylkusēt os, makēpet omen... Momusen ēyvpahyet esayat 'sayen mv uewv-hvsē-rakko likat eresorvtēs. Mohmet mv resorat, estvn mv hoktalat likētayat, Mvn liketskvrēs, kihcen, uewv onvpvn ohliken... Momusen mvn mēcvra-nen okvtētok, svokv hayēcet, 'mvyvhiken vyępen... Momusen mv uewv sēhoneckat aknvrkvpv mahen uewv oksētkē tvlket estvmąhen ossicet omen kaken vrępet ohmvtet... Mi uewv aknvrkvpv 'tan afvnket omen, epuse tat hēcet hvkihket ohliken... Vkueket atet mv epuse ohlikat elecu-san yvfvnket omis 'punvkv tat omylkvn ehosēpvtēt omehpvtet... Atet, yosiyet epuse yohtakhaket ohwakket hvkihket omētok turopuswv ocēt ohwakket omisat... Momusen ąyet mv uewv akhvtvpkē pokēpan vtękuset, mv hoktvlē ohlikvtē vtēkat fakke estahcet, mv hoktalat mv uewv-hvsē holattat akcehyet sumkehpen, Ervtēpvyvntvs, makesasvtēs maket onahoyvnts cē. Monkv epuse tat ēyvpvyēpvtēs kometvt omvnts.

He had almost forgotten how to talk, but he could still talk a little, and that partner of his [the snake] talked to him: Are you leaving now? he asked... I thought about it. Whatever is going to happen, I came because I want to see you for the last time and then leave, he said... It has happened, [the snake] said as he cried, and unable to do anything, he talked to [the man] as he sat in the water he had created himself. He talked with him, saying, My grandmother must come, if only just to see me. Bring her back with you and she'll see me. And when you come, my grandmother must sit on the bank right above the water. And you must sit apart shaking a rattle and singing, and when I'm ready I'll come out, he said... Then slowly he entered the big lake and his partner returned [home].

And as he said, he came back, and kept going until he got to where the grandmother of the young man who'd turned into a snake lived, and told her what had happened. After he had spoken, the old lady sat and cried... Wherever this place is, I must go see him, she said... Then he took her and came to the big lake. And when they reached there, where the old woman might sit, he said, You will sit there, and she sat above the water... Then as he'd been told to do, he shook a rattle and sang for a while... Then near the middle of the dangerous water, [the snake] made great troughs appear, but they remained seated... At a distance he sur-faced near the middle of the water, and his grandmother, seeing him so hideous, sat and cried... Moving forward, he came out right below where his grandmother was sitting, but he'd lost his ability to speak... He came out and lay across his grandmother, and because he was crying he had tears in his eyes as he lay there... Then after a while, he began going back down into the water, and as soon as he had gone down completely, he broke the ground [leading] up to where the old lady sat, and after the old lady had disappeared into the blue waters, I came home, someone said, it's been told. So it is believed that he took his grandmother with him.

11

Man defeats a giant lizard

Members of a hunting party disappear one by one until only one remains. He discovers a giant lizard has been capturing the others. When the lizard chases the man, he stuffs a tobacco twist in its mouth and kills it. Then he finds that all the others have been killed and returns home.

Giant lizards often appear in Creek and other southeastern stories, occurring in this collection in stories 11, 16, and 26.

Fayvlket vpēyvtēs. Este vnvcumēt fullet vpēyvtēs. Mont fullet omvtētan, hopvyēn eroricet omen, hvpo hayvkēt vpoket fayat fullvtēs.

Mont oman fayvranet ayē vtēkat sumkēpvtēs. Momen vyẹ̄pen sụlkēt ful-let omvtētan poyēpvtēs. Momen mv fayvlke sulkē fullvtē hvmkusēt vhoskvtēs. Mont vkerricet taklikvtēs. Mont vkerricet respoyat, Vne mahvkvts ci, mahket ayvtēs. Moman ēkvnv estv fvccvn ayē vtēkat, sumkēt omvtē kērrēt omvtēs. Mont omet mv vpēhoyē este sumēcvtē mv fvccvn ayvtēs.

Mont aret hopvyē 'svheremahekon, este nake vyocēpet omvtēt nene-paskē omēt nake sufotēcis 'svpēhoyēs. Momēt nene omēt wakken eshēcvtēs.

Mont mvn ervpihket ayof, taksvpulkv-rakkot omēpvtētut vlaken hecvtēs. Momis mv este eseko monken hehcet este tawvt hēcvtēs. Mont momusen enlētkvtēs. Momis mv este pvfne-mahēt omvtēs. Mont enletkēpet 'svrẹ̄pvtēs. Estomehcet emontvlē tayat mvn momēcetvn komet onkv 'svrẹ̄pvtēs. Momen mv taksvpulkv-rakko mv este ēsvyē tvlket komēpet omēpekv mvo wikeko tayusvtēs. Mont omis mv taksvpulkv-rakko tat hotusēpvtēs. Momen mv esteu mvo hotusepē hakvtēs. Momis mv este ēyapohicēpusēt omvtēs. Monkv emontvlē tayet omat kerrētatēs.

Momen taksvpulkv-rakko tat hvwạklusē hakēt omen mv este hēcvtēs. Mon omet mv este lētkē arat ayet eto rakkēt hueren ervfulotkat mvn fekhonnvtēs. Mont omat mv este hece-opiken rakkē hẹ̄ren ēpikēt omvtēs.

Some hunters went hunting. Several men went. And in going about, they soon had gone very far, so they made camp, settled in, and hunted daily.

Now each time a hunter went out to hunt, he would disappear. And as time went on, nearly all of the hunters were gone. And out of the many hunters, only one was left. And he sat and thought. And after he had thought about it, he said, It could happen to me, and took off. Then he knew that no matter what direction he took, he would get lost. So he took the direction that the missing hunters had taken.

Before he went very far, it looked like the thing that had been catching humans had cleared a path by dragging things along. Thus he found what appeared to be a road.

As he entered [the road], he saw a big mountain boomer coming.* But before it caught the man, the man saw it first. And he immediately started running from it. The man was a very fast runner. And he kept running as if it were a game. He was thinking as he ran of what he could do to defeat it. Now the big lizard was thinking only of catching the man, so it wouldn't stop, either. But the big lizard was getting very tired. And the hunter, too, was getting tired. The hunter was disciplined, though. So he knew he could defeat it.

Now the man saw that the big lizard had its mouth wide open in exhaustion. Then the running man went around a big tree and stopped on the other side. The hunter had a large twist of tobacco in his pocket. And he

* The word *taksvpulkv* is an uncommon term for a type of lizard. The late George Bunny (personal communication) used *taksvpulkv-rakko* for the mountain boomer or Eastern collared lizard (*Crotaphytus collaris collaris*), a large, pugnacious lizard (occasionally as large as fourteen inches) that sometimes runs on its hind legs.

Mont omet mvn erisēm ehakvtēs. Momen mv taksvpulkv-rakko tat hotusēpet ont omis, mv esten ēsvyē tvlket komet omēpekv, mvo wikeko tayet omis, hotusepē hēret omvtēs. Momen mv este em etetakēt 'mehakusēt mv eto pvlhvmken huerēpvtēs.

Momen mv taksvpulkv-rakko hvwaklat estvmahen mv eto mv este vhueran rvfulotkof, mvn huerēpvtet mv hece-opike-rakkon ecukwvn 'sem vsekē-yvtēs. Mohmet mvn 'semontalvtēs. Mont 'saret mv taksvpulkv-rakko tat mvn emontahlet elēcvtēs.

Mont elehcof, Estvn este sumēcvtē mvn vpoyet aret omētok mvn hecvyē tayē ont os, kohmet ayvtēs. Mv taksvpulkv-rakko atē hēcvtē fvccvn ayvtēs. Mont ayet mv taksvpulkv-rakko atvtē fvccvn ayet omaten, cvto-rakko ocvkēt omen ayet mvn eroran, mv cvto ocan, mv este sumēcvtē mvn omylkvt lumhen ereshēcvtēs. Mont omis mvn vyocet omylkvn pvsvtē poyepen omēpekv estomeko tayvtēs. Momis mv este-vyocv tat mv hvmkusē vhoskatet mv nake holwvyēcv elehcet mv enhvmkuset vhosket omvtētok, mv enhvmkuset encuko ervlaket: Nake momēt tayen este yvmakkuecēpen ont omis, vnhvmkuset vcvhosket ervlaket omis, maket mv em etvlofv rvlakvtēs, mahokvnts cē.

waited for it with [the tobacco]. Though the big lizard was very tired, it was thinking only of catching the man, so it, too, would not stop even though it was very, very tired. And the hunter was ready, waiting for it, and stood hidden on the other side of the tree.

Now when the big lizard with its mouth wide open went around the tree where the man stood, the man standing there took the big tobacco twist and stuffed it in its mouth. And that is how he defeated the big lizard. And that is how he defeated it and killed it.

And having killed it, he wanted to see where it had put all the missing men and decided to go look. He went in the direction from which he'd seen the big lizard come. And going in the direction from which the big lizard had come, he came upon some big rocks, and going further, where the rocks were, he found all the missing men lying there. And because it had caught and killed them all, he could do nothing. The evil thing that caught the men was killed by the one remaining man, and as he was all by himself, he returned home alone: Something has happened, something killed all the hunters and I've come home alone, he said as he returned to his town, they used to say.

12

Man races a snake

A joker implores his friends to tell him where a blue racer is so he can race it. Finally they tell him, and he gets the snake to chase him. The man is able to kill the snake by jumping over and under a fallen tree so that the snake becomes entwined (cf. Swanton 1929, Creek story 22).

Este hvmket okhacē hērēt arvtēs. Mont omaten cetto-pafnvt svsēt omvtēs. Mont omen mv este okhacē arat mv cetto-pafnv ēyassēcepickvn eyacēt aret omen, mv 'metohkvlketvt 'mvsēhakvtēs. Mvo fayētat fullēpet omhoyen, mv este okhacat mvn est vcak-aret omen okhoyvtēs. Momis hacohakēt omēpet okēpekv, Estvn mv nake aret monkat liken hēcacken omat, vm onvyvkvccvs, maket aret omvtēs. Momen 'saret, Estomvranet on maket 'saret oken omat, momvranat tvlkan omēs, kicahket 'mvsēhakvtē wikvkēpvtēs. Mont estit naken kicekon vrēpet omvtēs. Momis mvn komēpē hērēt vrēpet okēpet onkv, mvn 'sēnaoricēt arē monkvtet... Mv fayvlke fayē fullakvtē yvtelokaket estomē fullat onvyaket omen, tak-vpohoken ayen hvmket okat, Vne tat nake hecvkot arit omvyisan, cetto-pafnvt liken hehcis maket onayen... Mv este mvn pohetv yacat elēpē ont takliket oman ohken... Momusen, Estvmin liket on omat lvpkēn rvm onvyaks, maket vrēpen... Kos! Mvtis em vsēheyēt ont omis, ēmet momēn eyacēpat okēpētok 'svpehyet rem onvyaks. 'Saret ē esepicekvs, kicaket... 'Senhomēcakat sasen, momen momvrē eyacekat saset omis, momis hvtvm estomēcen hecetv eyacateu sasvtēs.

Mont mv cetto hēcē arat tat esayvtēs. Estvn mv cetto likēt omat onvyvranat ayvtēs. Momen mvn okēpekv mv este tat afvckē tatēs.

Mont echv-kotaksen ocepēt omvtēs. Momet reu sulkēt vpvkēn omvtēs. Mont mv cetto likat ervwolicēn omat, hvte eroricēko monken, em ete-takehpin, eroh-vpeyeyvrēs maket omen, mvn em ehakēt es fullet onkv. Mv cetto likat ervwolicet omen... Yvmv tut omēpis, kicet omhoyen... Momusen mon omat, em etetakehpin omvkēts, maket omen, 'mehaho-ken... Vrēpet em etetahket: Tokvs ca! ē maket vrēpen... Momusen oh-vpēyvtēs. Mon vpēyet ervwolēn eroricen, Mvn omis, kicet rem

There once was a man who was a real joker. In those times there were blue racers.* Now that man wanted to have a blue racer chase him, but his friends forbade him. They also were out hunting, and the joker had gone with them, so they cautioned him. But being crazy, he said, Tell me if you see that thing going about or sitting someplace, he said. And they said, Whatever he wants to do with it, he is going to do, so they stopped cautioning him. No one said anything to him. But he really wanted it badly, so all his efforts were to make it happen... The hunters came in from hunting and were telling about their hunt, and as they sat around, one hunter said, I didn't see a thing, but then I came upon a blue racer sitting there, he told them... The joker had been sitting around dying to hear that... Quickly, he said, Hurry and tell me where it was... No! Even though we warn him, he still wants to do what he wants, so take him and show him. Let him get himself caught, they said... There were some who were aggravated with him, and there were those who didn't want it to happen, yet there were also those who wanted to see what he could do.

So the one who'd seen the snake took him. He went to show him where the snake was. And because this is what he wanted, the man was very happy.

Now he had a bow. And he had many arrows with it. When we get close to where the snake is, just before we get there, let me get ready, and then we'll go on, he said, because they were waiting for him. They were getting close to where the snake was... It was right along here, he said to him... Then, if so, let me get ready, he said, and they waited... He got ready: Now! he said to himself as he went about... Then they went to [the place]. And as they got closer, That's where it was, they told him... Well,

* The expression *cetto-pafnv* sounds like a specific type of fast snake. Margaret Mauldin has heard this term used for a snake called a 'blue racer'.

onahohyen... Momusen, Mon omat enletkvranit omis, maket aret, oh-
ayat, ayet eroren, mv cetto likat rvwolēn eroret, erem pahiken... Moman
vtękusen, mv cetto tat, mvn komepvtēt likēpet oman ohken... Momusen
mv cetto tat mv este asiyen, mv este tat mvn okvtētok, enletiken 'svhoyat...
Mv este tat pohkusat pihket sumkat... Hvtvm pihket eratvcokat hēckusen,
pihket hoyanen omat, vcewē haken mv este yayat mahusan ohhueret mv
cetto tat estvmahet lekvkappet wakket hoyanen... Mv esteu pihket mvo
hoyanen, eswelvkēpet omusymmvliken, momusen mv este tat vwolicē
hēret mv cetto tat eshoyanē haken eshoyvnhoyvtēs. Momis mv este tat
estomēs konko ont—enhomahtet 'svrēpet ont omis, mv cetto mit mv
esten vwolicē hēret eshoyanvtēs.

Momen vyusymmvliken, mv este tat momusen eto tis tulkvtē toheksē tis
wakkvnto oman, mvn hecepēt mv este aret omēpvtet, momusen mv cetto
tat cakkētt omen, momusen mv este tat mv eto toheksan retohtaskvtēs.
Mont mvn 'mehaken—mv cetto tat mvn roret onkv, esvranē tvlkē 'sem
mont, mv cetto mvo, matvpont ervwvlapket on omis... Mv este mv eto
toheksan elecvn raropottehpen, hvtvm mv cetto mvo matvpont omis, mv
cettot cvpkēt onkv, estonko tayet, mv eton vpvllvkētt omen... Momusen
mv este tat mvn em eteropottet momof mv cetto vpvllaket estonko tayē
haket vyēcicen... Momusen mv este tat mv eto 'tohtaskē vtēkat, rahvtēs.
Mont hvtvm pvlhvmkē erorat mvo, rahvtēs.

Mon ayen mv cetto momusen emontalvtēs. Mont esvrēpet elēcvtēs. Mon
mvn okēpvtētok, Mvn momēcvyētut okvyētvnks, maket vrēpvtēs,
mahokvnts cē.

all right, then. I'm going to run from it, he said, and went toward it until
he was there, and being very close to where the snake was, he whooped...
As soon as he did, the snake was sitting ready for something like this...
Then the snake chased the man, and because the man had wanted this, he
began to run from it [with the snake following]... The man could barely
be heard whooping, then fading in the distance... As he returned, he would
be whooping as he came into sight and would run past, and after a long
time, exactly where the man had passed, the great, shining snake went
by... The man kept whooping as he passed by, and after they did this a
long time, the snake began passing by right behind the man as they went
by. But the man didn't care—he was in the lead as they went, but the
snake was getting very close to the man as they passed by.

They kept this up until finally [they came to where] the man had earlier
spotted a tree that had fallen down and was lying there as if propped up,
and because the snake was catching up with him, the man jumped over
the fallen tree. Then he waited—the snake came thinking it would catch
him, and crossed over the tree the same way... The man came back
through under the fallen tree, and again the snake did the same, but
because the snake was long, it couldn't do anything, and had wrapped
itself around the tree... Then the man went through back and forth many
times, and the snake became entwined and could no longer do anything...
Then every time the man jumped over the tree, he shot it. When he
reached the other side, he would shoot at it again.

After a while, he overcame the snake. He finally killed it. And as he had
said [he would do], he went around saying, I said I could do it, they used
to say.

13

Rabbit traps Lion on the other side of the ocean

Lion boasts that he has devoured everyone in the west. Rabbit lies that he has done the same in the southeast. To test their boasts, Rabbit proposes that they see who can pass human bones. When Lion's eyes are shut, Rabbit switches the piles so that it appears he has passed human bones and Lion has only passed little round lumps. Lion says he makes the sound "Say, say, say, say, say, say" when he sleeps. Rabbit boasts that he says "Big Chief Toh-Thlo-Tok!" Rabbit feigns sleep; when Lion is asleep, Rabbit dusts him with hot ashes. Lion chases him back and forth across a small creek which Rabbit magically widens, stranding Lion on the other side (cf. Swanton 1929, Creek story 43).

As in the other stories, Rabbit is so cunning that he completely dominates more powerful animals. This story is well known and old, and shows knowledge that lions live across the ocean.

Cufet, momen Este-Papvn 'tenrapvtēs. Este-Papvt hvse-aklatkv fvccvn atet, aret okatet,

Hvse-aklatkv elecv cuko tat vntvntaken vlakis,

maket yvhikēpen, Cufet pohvtēs. Momet momusen Cufe tat nak fone towēn hopot mvn wvnvkēn etakkayehpet,

Hvse-ossv elecv cuko vntvntaken yvn vlakis,

makē tat yvhiket Este-Papvn ervnrapvtēs. Mont eretehēcet omen 'tem punahoyvtēs.

Mont Este-Papvt okat, Hvse-aklatkv tat este poyit atet omis, kicen... Cufeu matvpomēn, Vneu Hvse-ossv elecv este poyit atit yvn vlakit omis, kicvtēs.

Momof Cufet okat, Mon omat estit este fone eshoyvnepē tayen omat kērrvkēs, kicen... Momepekvs, kicvtēs. Momen Cufet okat, Musoholēt omvkvrēs, kicvtēs. Momepekvs, kihcet em vkvsamvtēs. Momen momusen hokkolvt 'metetahket kaken... Este-Papv tat musǫlusēt likvtēs. Momen Cufe tat renayēt likvtēs. Mont mv este-papv hoyanat, este fone ţlkusēn hoyanet oman, Cufe tat cerēhusēn hoyanet omet, ēme mv momē hoyanan acawet mv este-papvn iem vpoyet esliket omet, ēme tat mv este-papv hoyanan, acawet ēme likat elecvn avpoyet... Cufe tat likēpet, tạyē oricehpet... Hokvs! Cufet kihcen, hokkolvt asehohket hecakan... Mv este-papv likvtē tat, nake cerēhusēt vpoken hēcvtēs. Mont okat cvmǫmusēs kǫmvkatētan, mucv vnnettv vwolvcoks cē, maket arvtēs.

Momen hvtvm 'tepahket vhoyvtēs. Mont vhoyen, yafken ernochoyvranet omen... Cufet okat, Heyvt Tohfokakv Hvccet os, kicvtēs. Mont omen

Rabbit and Lion met while going about. Lion came from the west, singing,

In the southwest all the houses were empty as I came here,

and Rabbit heard him. Rabbit hunted for bones, tied them together, and placed them on the ground:

In the southeast all the houses were empty as I came here,

he also sang and met Lion. Now having met each other, they talked together.

Then Lion said, I have come because I killed the people in the west... Rabbit, too, in the same way said, I, too, have come because I killed the people in the southeast.

Then Rabbit said, Let's find out who can pass human bones... Let it be so, [Lion] said. Then Rabbit said, Let's do it with our eyes closed. Let it be so, [Lion] said, agreeing. Right away both got ready and sat down... Lion sat with his eyes closed really tight. And Rabbit sat with his eyes wide open. Then when the lion passed, he passed only human bones, while Rabbit passed little round lumps, so [Rabbit] took what he had passed and placed them where the lion sat, and then he took what the lion had passed and put it under where he was sitting... Rabbit sat awhile, until he had enough... Now! Rabbit said, and both stood up and looked... Where the lion had sat, he saw little round lumps. And he said, I didn't think I would pass so little—my [dying] day is near, he said.

Then the two got together and went away. And as they were going, it was getting to be evening, and they were going to spend the night... Rabbit

mvn nochoyvranet onkv, momusen Cufe tat eto-hvrpen hopoyēpvtēs. Mon Este-Papvt okat, Estomēcvranet mv nake moman hopoyet ometske-haks? kicvtēs. Momen Cufet okat, Tạyen est etkolēt omvnken, 'tecarēs kont omis, kicvtēs. Mont Cufet Este-Papvn em pohet okat, Cenocat nak maket cenocēt omehaks? kicet em pohen... Este-Papvt okatet, Si, si, si, si, si, si, maket cvnocēt omvcoken okhoyētvnks, kicvtēs. Momen hvtvm Este-Papvt Cufen em pohet, Centv? Nak maket cenocēt omhaks? kicet Este-Papvt em pohen... Mēkko-rakko tohrotok! maket cvnocēt omēs kicvtēs. Momen takwakhoken, momusen Cufe tat nocepē omēt, mvn maket nocēt omvtē estem onayekv, Mēkko-rakko tohrotok, makēpen Este-Papv tat pohet takwakkvtet, momusen Este-Papv tat nocēpvtēs. Momis mv este-papv tat fvccvn maket nocēpet omēpet okekv, mv Si, si, si, si, si, si, maket nocēpet entakwakken...

Cufe tat alihket, momusen mv eto-hvrpe rakkusan enhopoyepēt takwvke-cēpvtet, mvn ēsso-hiye hēran eskēfet... Momusen mv este-papv wakkan ohpefiken, momusen Este-Papv tat cvpvkiket, atasiket, mv cufe tat as-sehcen 'svhoyvtēs.

Mon eswelaken hvccuce wakken Cufet 'metohtasken eswelaken... Mv hvccuce mv cufe tohtaskē vtēkat, Hvcce rakkvnto! kicet... 'Metohtaskat mv hvccuce rakkēn omēto estomis, mv este-papvo matvpon 'metohtasken eswelaken... Tvpalvn Cufet tiken Este-Papvo entiken... Hvtvm Cufe tat ratohtaskēpvtēs. Mohmen Este-Papvt ratohtaskeko tayen enhayēpvtēs. Cufet, mont omet Cufe tat atvpalvn vrēpet omet Este-Papv tat nak hayekot Cufe tat vrēpvtēs. Mon Este-Papv tat atiketv eyacet arvtēs, mv cufen enhomēcet assēcet 'saret omekv. Momis estonko tayet tvpalvn a aret omen... Wvko-rakkon enokwvn akwvkehcet atikvs! kicet, Cufe tat aret omen, Wvko-rakko enokwv akwvkēcet omis, aksumkēpen atikeko tayet... Momusen tvpalv-rakkon Cufet Este-Papvt tvyecicet omvtēs.

said, This is Tohfokaka River. And as this is where they would spend the night, Rabbit immediately began to gather tree bark. And Lion asked, What are you going to do with what you are gathering? Then Rabbit said, One gets very cold, so I thought I'd build a fire. Then Rabbit asked Lion, When you sleep, what kind of sound do you make? Lion said, They tell me I make the sound, Say, say, say, say, say, say when I sleep, he said. Then Lion asked Rabbit, What about you? What sound do you make when you sleep? When I sleep I say, Big Chief Toh-Thlo-Tok! he said. And they lay down to sleep, and then Rabbit pretended to be asleep and made the sounds that he had said, saying, Big Chief Toh-Thlo-Tok! Lion heard him as he lay there, and then Lion fell asleep. But the lion had spo-ken the truth, for as he fell asleep, he said, Say, say, say, say, say, say, and lay sleeping...

Rabbit got up and looked for the biggest piece of tree bark that he had placed by him, and shoveled hot ashes with it... Then he dusted the lion with them as he lay there, and Lion got very angry, jumped up, and chased the rabbit.

And as they went, Rabbit jumped over a small creek, and they kept going... Every time the rabbit jumped over the little creek, he'd say, River that gets big! As he jumped over, the creek would grow wider, but the lion would jump over the same way, and they continued on... Rabbit crossed to the other side, and Lion crossed, too... Rabbit jumped back across again. Then he made it so Lion could not jump back across. Rabbit was on this opposite side so he went about ignoring Lion. Lion wanted to cross back over, for he was very angry with the rabbit and still wanting to chase him. But there was nothing he could do on the opposite bank... Put the neck of a great blue heron in the water and come across! Rabbit said, and [Lion] put a heron's neck down, but it sank, and he could not cross... So Rabbit made Lion cross the ocean.

14

Rabbit seeks wisdom from God

Rabbit asks God for wisdom. God says Rabbit must first bring back an alligator. Rabbit tricks Alligator into revealing his weak spot and kills him. God then says to bring back a sack full of mosquitoes. Rabbit tells the mosquitoes he doesn't think they can fill up the sack, but they fill it, and he brings it back to God. God then demands that Rabbit bring back a rattlesnake. Under the ruse of measuring the rattlesnake with a stick, Rabbit kills him and brings him to God. God says that he could not possibly give him more cunning and condemns him to steal from gardens (cf. Swanton 1929, Creek stories 64–66).

This is the well-known story "The Tasks of Rabbit" (Swanton 1929; Bascom 1992), showing Rabbit's ability to outsmart any animal.

Cufet arvtēs, mahokvnts. Mont aret omet, hoporrenkvn ocēt ometvn eyacet aret omet, Hesaketvmesēn em pohvtēs. Mon Hesaketvmesēt okatet, Mon omat, vsin Vlpvtvt akwakkētok: mvn resvlaketsken omat, tan hoporrenkv cemarēs, kihcen... Ayat mvn Vlpvtv tat akwakken okhohyvten erem oret okatet, Hesaketvmesēt wakvn elēcvranet omet, Eshotupkvn vnwarekvs, cekicet oman arit omis kicvtēs. Momen mvn tayen aret okēs kohmet vcak-ayvtēs. Mont vcak-ayen vhoyen, mvn 'mvkeriyet elēcetvn eyacet 'saret okekv, 'sayen momusen 'svhopvyēcat nafkvtēs. Momis em elkv tokon ennafken, momusen Vlpvtv tat letkēpvtēs. Mont mv hvcce hvtvm yaktaskēpvtēs.

Momen mvn elēcekot letecihcet aret omen... Momen yem onayen Hesaketvmesēt okat, Resvlahketskē tvlken, hoporrenkv cemvranit ohkikv: mvn resvtetskeko vtēkat, cemvko tayet omes, kihohcen... Hvtvm yefulkvtēs, hoporrenkv oh-vpvkēn Cufe tat eyacet onkv. Mont aret hvtvm erem orvtēs. Mont eron ēhayēt eto uewv aakwiyēn erohcemket, fekēsket ohliken, Vlpvtv afvnkvtēs. Mont afvnket omen em punayet okat, Hesaketvmesēt wakvn elēcvranet omet, Eshotupkvn vnwarekvs, cekicet omen arit atet omis, kicen... Mvn maket tayen estenafket okhoyis, kicet omen... Momen cvcuset arēt omēs. Este hoporrēnesekot omētan mvn atotet omvcoken: Estvn momehcē witēs, maket omet... Erhecvs, mahoken arit omis, kicet enlaksen... Moman okēs enkohmet, hvtvm, vcak-atvtēs.

Momet welaken em pohet okat, Estvn cennafket ohmehaks? kicen... Cvkvn vnnafket ohs, kicen... Estvmvn cennafkate celēcvranvtētē? kicen... Cvsokson vnnafken omat, cvlēcvranvtēs, kihcet em onayvtēs. Mohmen mvn em onayekv, momusen mvn ennvfiket elēcēpvtēs. Mont

It was said there was a rabbit. And going about, he wanted to have wisdom and asked God. And God said, Very well, over yonder, Alligator is lying in the water: if you bring him back with you, I'll give you much wisdom, he said... [Rabbit] went and Alligator was lying there just as he had been told, and [Rabbit] said, I'm here because God is going to kill a cow and ordered you to cut the wood for roasting. And [Alligator] believed him and went with him. So he went with him, because Rabbit had tricked him and wanted to kill him... And when they had gone further, [Rabbit] struck [Alligator]. But he didn't hit him in the spot that would kill him, and immediately Alligator ran off. And he jumped back into the creek.

So not killing [Alligator], Rabbit let him run away... Then he came back and told God what happened, and God said, Only if you bring him back will I give you wisdom, as I said: as long as you do not bring him back, I can't give it to you, he told him... [Rabbit] went back again, because Rabbit did want more wisdom. So again he arrived [at Alligator's home]. Disguising himself as a squirrel, he climbed onto a limb out over the water, chattered there, and Alligator stuck his head out. So while his head was out of the water, Rabbit talked with him, saying, God is going to kill a cow, and I have come because he ordered you to cut the wood for roasting it... That's what they said just before I got beat up, [Alligator] said... I have a younger brother, [Rabbit said]. He is a very senseless person, yet [God] sent him, saying, He might do it somehow... I'm here because I was told to check on him, [Rabbit] said, lying to him... Believing what he said, [Alligator] went with him again.

Now as they were going along, [Rabbit] asked him, Where did he hit you? He hit my head, he said... Where would he have to have hit you in order to kill you? [Rabbit] asked... If he'd struck me on the hip, it would have killed me, [Alligator] told him. Then as soon as he had told him 'svrēpet resem vlakvtēs. Mvn momēcen hecetvn 'yacet Hesaketvmesēt omekv resem vlakvtēs.

Momen hvtvm okyehan sokcv facken resatetskat tạwvn hoporrenkv cemarēs, kicvtēs. Momen mvo ayvtēs, mv okyeha hopokv.

Mont aret mv nake sasan eroret okat, Hesaketvmesēt okat, Heyv sokcv fackēs, kicvyan, Fvcikekos, maken aret omis. Fvcikatskekon okehaks? kicen... Mv mọmusat fvckvraneyat tylkusēt os, kicaken... Mon omat vtehkatsken hecvkēs, kicen, sokcv em enhvlaten vtẹhket fvciket res enhoyanen, momusen esenwvnvyehpet resatvtēs. Mont 'saret resvlaken, Hvtvm vsin Cetto-Mēkkot likēs. Mvn hvtvm erehsetsken, hoporrenkv cemarēs, kicvtēs.

Mohmen hvtvm mvn ayvtēs. Eton enfvskēn esehpet ayvtēs. Mont aret mv Cetto-Mēkko likan erorvtēs. Mon okat, Hesaketvmesēt okat, Heyv eto tvckē ietetayēs, kicvyan, Ietetahyekos maken... Mon omat erahopo-hyit hecvranis mahkit atit omis, kicen... Ietetayē witvyēs komvyēs, kicvtēs. Momis ohmēs kicvyan, Monhkos maket omen atit omvyis... Monkv lvpotkēt wvkiketsken ecehopayvranis, kicen... Lvpọtkusēt wvkiken, momusen mvn em vkerrēt okekv, mvn ekvn mv eto fvskan esensekehyet, elehcet, resatet resem vlakvtēs.

Mon okatet, Estomē resemontvlēn hoporrenkv cemvko tayet [oman] aret oketskes. Monkv hoktvlvke nake vhockuce hayēpan, ennọkset hueretskvrēs, Hesaketvmesēt kicvtēt omen, mv Hesaketvmesē nake kicvtēn ohhueret omet, mv omēcicēn tạyen nak vhockuce nokset omistvnts maket onahoyvnts cē.

that, [Rabbit] struck him [on the hip] and killed him. And he finally brought him back for [God]. This is what God wanted to see him do, so he returned bringing him [the alligator].

Now then, bring me a sack full of mosquitoes, and I will give you wisdom, [God] said. Then he went again, to hunt for the mosquitoes.

And he went to a place where they were plentiful and said, I said they could fill this bag, but God said, They couldn't fill it up, so that's why I'm here. Can you not fill this sack? he asked... We can surely fill that little thing up, they said... Well, then, let's see you get into it, he said, and held the sack open for them, and as soon as they got in and filled it to overflowing, he tied the sack and brought it back. And when he returned with it, [God] said, Now Rattlesnake lives over yonder. Go get him and I will give you wisdom.

So again off he went. He took a thorn from a tree and went. He went until he came to where Rattlesnake lived. Then he said, When I said you would be the same length as this piece of wood, God said you would not be the same length... Well, then, I'll go find one and see, I said, and that's why I've come, he said [to Rattlesnake]... I think I may be the same length, he said. When I said, I think they might be the same, [God] said, It would not be, so that's why I have come... So lie straight and I'll measure you, he said... He lay very straight, and this being a trick, [Rabbit] took the tree thorn, pierced his head, killed him, and brought him back [to God].

[God] said, There is no way I can give you more cunning than you have. So when the old women make a garden, you will always steal from the garden, God said, and God has stood by what he said to him, and for that reason [Rabbit] steals much from the garden, it's been told.

15
Two boys become thunder

A lion kills a pregnant woman and takes the baby out. The father teaches the child to use a bow, but he keeps losing them. The child reveals that a thicket child takes them, and this child comes to live with them. The father warns them to look out for Sharp Hoof, but they disobey. Sharp Hoof attacks, but they kill it, cut off its nose, and make a pipe out of it. When the father smokes it, it makes a noise and he knows it's not good. Then he warns them about Thunder's eggs. The children disobey and look for the eggs. When they touch them, the boys become thunder, one real and one false.

The false boy in this story is sometimes called Fvccv-seko *('truthless') in Creek (Swanton 1929:2–7), though the story is known to folklorists as "Lodge Boy and Thrown-Away" (Swanton 1929; Lankford 1987:160–75). Sharp Hoof goes by the name of* Kososop-Cvpko *('long nails') in Swanton (1929:6), a term Lankford (1987:253) relates to Choctaw bone-pickers. From other stories, it seems that the idea of two thunders, one real and one false, is a reference to thunder and lightning (Swanton 1929: 227–30; Jumper 1994:83). In other southeastern legends, Thunder Beings are thought to cause sickness (Grantham 2002:34).*

Este hvmket likvtēs. Momet ehiwv estuce ocvranēn omvtēs. Mont omat mv este honvnwv fakvn tąyēt omvtēs. Mont fakv vyēpat arętt eco 'lēcēt ervlaket vrępēt omvtēs. Mont omvtētut fakv ayvtēs.

Mont ayēt vrępvtet rvlvkekon este-papvt erem orvtēs. Mv este ehiwv tąlkusēt cuko estaklíken mont eremoret okat, Mv estuce ocvranetskat iecemēsvyēs, kicvtēs. Mont omis em vkvsvmekatēs. Momis mv este-papv tat vwicēcekot estakliket mv hoktē estuce iem esēpvtēs. Ecke tat elēcehpet, mv estuce hesakusēt omen... *Pvrken* kicēt ocakvtēs. Mvn ocvten mv estuce tat mvn vpihket topv elecvn eswvkehcet ecke tat 'svyēpvtēs.

Mon mv este honvnwv vrępvtet rvlakvtēs. Moman nake momēt omēpvten rvlaket taklikvtēs. Momen estuce omēt nak mąkē ont omat topv elecv oman okēpen rahēcan, mvn estuce tat pvrke vpikēt eswakket oken eshēcvtēs. Momet eraesēpvtēs. Moman cēpvnusēt omēpen vcayēcepēt vfvstēpet, estaklikēpet omvtētan, mv cēpvnusat vculicepusē hakēpet eccv-kotakse 'svrēpē hakepusēt ont omen... Eccv-kotaksuce enhayvntut fakv vyēpat vrępet rvlakat, mv eccv-kotaksuce ocepekot aren rvlaket ēti ton, tąn enhayet ont omis, sumecicepē ąlken fakv ayat rvlakēt omvtēs. Mont ont em pohvtēs: Eccv-kotakse cenhayvyat estomēcēt ometskehaks? kicvtēs. Mon mv cēpvnusat okat, Vsi hvfvpan cēpvnēt arēt omat, Vnet cecuset omis, maket arēt ont omet, mvt vm esēpēt os, kicvtēs.

Momen vyēpen, mv estuce hvfvpat arē kicvtē vcak-aten vlahokvtēs. Mon mv hokkolan takkayēpet eslikvtēs. Mont okat, Laksv-Fvske hocefkēt likēt omēs. Estvn rem orhohyatskēs: mv tąn vhohyatskvs, kicet omvtēs. Moman mv hvfvpē-estucet okat, Laksv-Fvske encuko vhoyvkvccvs maket okhoyekisa? kicen... Kos, mvn vhohyatskvs maket okhohs,

There once lived a man. And his wife was going to have a baby. Now the man was a very good hunter. He would go hunting, kill a deer, and bring it home. This being his custom, he went hunting.

Now he was out awhile and had not returned when a lion came to his house. The man's wife was home alone, and when [the lion] got there he said, I can take out that baby you're going to have for you. But she didn't give him permission. But the lion would not give up and finally took the baby out of the woman. He killed the mother, though the baby was barely alive... There used to be [split-cane baskets] called *pvrke*. He found one, put the baby in it, put it under the bed, and took the mother away.

The man finally came home. He came home to this situation and sat down. Then he heard sounds like a baby from underneath the bed, and when he went to look, he found the baby lying in the split-cane basket. Then he took the baby out. The baby was a boy and he took very good care of him, and as time went by, the little boy grew a little older and learned to use the bow... The father would make him a little bow and would go hunting, but when he returned, the boy would not have the little bow, so he'd make another one every time, and [the boy] would lose it every time the father returned from hunting. So he asked him: What do you do with the little bows I make for you? Then the little boy said, Over there in the thicket is a boy who says, I'm your younger brother, and he's the one who takes it from me.

Then as time passed, the younger child spoken of in the thicket came back with the boy. [The man] took him in and cared for them both. And he told them, There is someone by the name of Sharp Hoof living around here. You might go there by mistake: do not go there, he said. But the thicket baby said, Weren't we told to go to Sharp Hoof's house? No, we

kicvtēs. Mv este-mahhucet kicet, em vyeko tayēt omvtēs. Momen vculv-
kusē hakē ayat, vcak-ayet welvkępat mv nake Laksv-Fvske hocefkē likat
vhoyvtēs. Momet rem orhoyet omen, Nake herękusēt ocēt os.
Yecvwepaks, kicet mv Laksv-Fvske tat liket omen, momusen eccv-
kotaksucen ocet oken mvn em eyacakvtēs. Mont oh-vhoyvtēs. Mont mv
eccv-kotakse cvwehpet erastokorken... Mv Laksv-Fvske tat elaksvn
asēchet omat, mvttecihcet eto min vcakhēcet vliken yohtokoriket rahet
elēcakvtēs. Mohmet eyupon entahcet resvthoyvtēs. Mont mv resvthoyof
okakat, Cerken rvlaken omat, Heyvn hecepakwvn cenhayet omēs,
kiceyvrēs, kicakvtēs.

Mont mv erke rvlvkekon rvlahoket, momet mv Laksv-Fvske eyupo
resvlahoket wvkecaken mv erke ervlakvtēs. Momen mvn okakekv, Papv,
hecepakwvn cenhayeyvnks, kicakvtēs. Moman ravm esaks cē. Esmok-
kicvranis, kicvtēs. Momen riem esakvtēs. Mon esmokkicet omat, Cek-
Cek, maken... Nake herekon omet okatskes. Vsin 'svhohyet ervwikvkes,
kihcen 'svhohyet rvwikakvtēs. Momen hvtvm vsin Tenētkē echustaket
ocēt omēs. Mvo celahyatskvs. Tenētkēt encakēt omēs. Monkv herekot
omēs, kicvtēs. Moman mv hvfvpē-estucet okat, Vsin Tenētkē echustaket
ocēt omēs, maket, Mvn riencvwvkvccvs, cerke maket okekisa? kicet
omen... Mvo makekot, mvn celahyatskvs. Herekot omēs maket okhohs,
kicet mvo 'meyacekatēs. Momis mvo vwicēceko tayen momusen encem-
hokvtēs. Mont mv tenētkē custake encvwakvtēs. Momen mv momē nake
celayakan, naket cawvtēs. Momen mvt mv estucvlke tatēt hvlwē catēt
mvt tenētkat estet omistvnts, mahokvnts cē. Hvmket fvccv sekot omen,
hvmket este-mahhucet omēs. Monkv tenētkē hokkolet omēs cē.

were told not to go there, [the real boy] said. The real boy always said
that, and would not go there. Then as they grew older, always being
together, they went to where the thing named Sharp Hoof lived. When
they got to his place, Sharp Hoof said, Here are some very pretty things.
Come and get them, he said as he sat, and they saw he had some little
bows that they very much wanted. So they went toward them. And they
took the little bows and ran back with them... That Sharp Hoof shot himself at them with his hooves, but he missed, got stuck on a tree, and was
trying to get out when they ran back and shot him dead. Then they cut off
his nose and brought it back. And as they were bringing it back, they
said, When your father comes home we'll say, We've made you a pipe.

Now the father had not returned when they got there, and they brought
Sharp Hoof's nose back and laid it down, and then the father came home.
Then they said to him, Papa, we've made a pipe for you. Well, go get it
for me. I want to smoke with it, he said. So they went and got it. And
when he was smoking with it, it said, Chek-Chek... You have something
here that's not good. Take it over there and throw it away, he said, and
they took it and threw it away. Now over there are Thunder's eggs. Do
not touch those, either. Thunder is possessive of them. Therefore it's not
a good thing, [the father] said. But the thicket baby said, Your father said
Thunder's eggs are over there. Didn't he say that we should get them? he
asked... He didn't say that, [the real boy] said, he said, Don't touch them.
It's not good, he replied, and wouldn't agree. Even so, [the thicket baby]
wouldn't stop, so they began climbing for them. And they took the thunder
eggs. And because they handled them, something got them. And when
those that were babies are thundering in the red sky, it used to be a human,
it was said. One is false and one is a real baby. So there are two thunders.

16

Tiger helps man defeat a giant lizard

A hunter's dogs find a giant lizard, and the lizard takes them off one by one. The hunter runs back toward camp but is caught in its mouth. A tiger appears, defeats the lizard, and helps the hunter, but he says that the hunter must protect his children, the cat and the bobcat. One day the hunter sees a cat stalking a turkey. The cat pounces and dislodges an eyeball. The hunter asks if he's all right, but the cat jerks out the eyeball and runs off (cf. Swanton 1929, Creek story 20).

Margaret Mauldin says, "We were always told that if you kill a coyote, you shouldn't travel alone at night." Animals occur in clans and members of clans respond to you based on your past behavior. You should fulfill your obligations even if your help is rejected.

Fayet aresasvtēs. Mont fayēpat vrēpēt omvtēs, hopvyēn. Momēt vrēpēt omvtētan, nake punvttv tat pvsvtēpet... Momet hvtvm efvn sulkēn omvtēs. Momet mv efv tat efv fayvlket omekv, nak punvttuce tąyen pvsvtēpēt omvtēs. Mont aret omvtētan, efv tat estvn nak wohēcēto vtēkat, nake punvttvn oken mv efv-pucase enkerrēt omvtēs.

Mont onkv esayvtēs, fayepvranat. Mont ayat vrēpet nak elēcet omis ayē monken hvtvm efv tat seksēkusat esvpokacoken, momusen mv efv-pucase tat, vlece mahēt ayat, ąyet eroran, cvto-rakko estvmahet oman, mv mahen okēpen... Ąyet eroran, taksvpulkv-rakkot vrēpen eshecaket okehpvtet ont omis, mv efv sulkat hvmke-ylken esepvntut ehutet omacoks komvkat mahe tat resvsumket hofonekvnton efv tat yesēpet esvrēpen okvkehpvten hēcet huervtet, momusen ehvpo fvccvn eralētkvtēs. Mont eratet oman, mv efv wohkakvte cvyayvkē omē haken em apohicvntut... Ayusē hayen momusen efv tat hvtvm em apohican, efv tat cvyąyakus hakēpen ayen omat momusen mv nake efv vyocē, 'sarē hehcē rienlētkat, mvt hvtvm mv efv-pucasen assēcēpat... Ayusē hayen cvcakkēpen hēcv-yvntvs, makvtēs, mahokvnts. Mont omis vneu ayusē hayin, vtēpet, momusen cvcvkiket momusen cvsēpvntvs, makesasvtēs. Momen cvsēpet omēpekv, yescvfulket omen ont omis, momusen estomvko tayet vtvtąrkin momusen 'svcvyēpvntvs.* Momen 'svcayet omisan hvtvm nake oklanē omēt nekēyen hēcit omvyis, mvn hvtvm hvmket aret omētvlkētok... Mvn eretepaken omat, momusen, Cvstomēcepvranēs, komvken vtarkvyvntvs. Mont omen 'svcayet omisan, Yvmv mąhen nake tat nekēyet os komvken, mimv min vkerricet vtąrkin omisan, mvn nake vrēpet ohmvtet... Mvn resvcoren kaccvt vrēpet omehpvtet... Mv taksvpulkv-rakkon enhomecepēt vrēpet ohmvtet, momusen mvn ohtasiket hosken... Vrusē hat momusen mv vne cvcokpikvtē acvwihket, momusen mv kaccv min hvtvm ietepoyetv eyacacoket aret omis, mv kaccv tat entvhopkēn 'semontvlē hērēt onkv

* The word vtvtąrkin should probably be vtąrkin.

Someone was hunting. He went hunting in faraway places. He went continually, killing small game... And he had many dogs. And the dogs were hunting dogs, so he had killed many animals. When hunting, he always knew his dogs had an animal trapped by the sound of their barking.

So it was that he took them on a hunt. He would go and kill animals, and as he went, all his dogs began barking frantically in one location, so the dogs' master walked very fast until he came to a place where there were huge boulders, and that was about where they were as he approached... They had found a giant lizard, but from the many dogs, the lizard was taking one dog at a time and disappearing, and before long it would return for another dog, he saw, standing there, and then he ran back toward his camp. As he came back, he listened occasionally and heard the dogs gradually cease their barking... As he continued on, he kept listening for the dogs but they had grown quiet and the creature that he had seen catching the dogs began chasing the dog's master... I saw it catching up to me, he said, it was said. I kept going, but it caught me, he said. Having caught me, it was taking me back, but unable to do anything, I just hung there as it took me. As he was taking me, I saw something sort of brown moving, and I assumed it was another one... When the two get together, Something will happen to me, I thought as I hung there. As he continued taking me, all I could think about was, This is right where something moved, and I hung there, and indeed it had been another creature... As [the lizard] carried me there, it became clear that it had been a tiger...† It had been going around angry with the giant lizard, and immediately jumped on the lizard and began scratching him... After a while, the lizard dropped me from its mouth and wanted to fight the tiger back, but because the tiger was more

† The word kaccv is interpreted by Creek speakers in Oklahoma as 'tiger', but in Florida as the Florida panther (a type of mountain lion or puma).

estohmen estomēceko tąyuset... Mv kaccv tat aohtasiket hoskat, hvtvm taskat eto cvpv min ervliket ehvcen nekēyicet vlikvtet... Rataskat hvtvm mv kaccv hoskvntut, taskat mvn momet omēpisekv, eto vcvpv min vlikēpen... Mv nake casē arat on omat momusen emontvlket vyēpen, mv kaccv tat naket estomvt sekon entvhopkē emonkusen... Vrēpet omet 'svrēpet momusen emontahlet mv nake tat momusen caset omet, Ehuten 'svcayet omē tvlkēs, komvket omisat, mv kaccv hvteceskv hoskē 'sarē ervcvwikat nekēyvyesekut wakkin eswelvkēpet omisan... Mv taksvpulkv-rakko tat momusen emontahlacoken mv nake casē 'svcarvtē tat cvwihket hvlvlątket atat fvccv tat rvsumiken momusen, momusen mv kaccv tat aatet vlaket cvhēcet yehueret omisan, vm punayet okat, Celekis omehaks? maket omis, mvo 'svm vpvyetvn komet okat tvlkēs komit, omis nak kįcv-yesekut, wakkin okatet... Celekon omat, cem vnicvranit okis cē. Alikvs. Alihket hvse-ossv fvccvn vhecēt likvs, cvkihcen... Alihket, hvsossv fvc-cvn vhecvyēt lihkin vcvfulotket aret ostihcet... Momusen acvcokokvs, maket omen... Kos, cvhonnepusēt omēs, kicvyan, momis 'Svm estonhkos. Eco honvntake tis acukoyit vm vretvt os. Monkv naket 'svm estomemahekot vm vretvt os. Monkv acvcokokvs, cvkicet omen, momusen acokohkin, 'svcayat mv nake cvsē 'svcatat mąhusate-ylken 'svcayet omisan... Mv hvteceskv mv nake ercasan resvcoran, eccv tis vm vwiken wakkvten... Heyvn eccvt wakket os. Mvn nake cenake tokat omehaks? makisan... Mvt eccv cvnaket os, kicin... Mon omat aesepvs, cvkihcen aesehpin... Hvtvm rē-hotvwvn hvtvm eslikvten... Hvtvm mvn cenaket omekohaks? maken... Hēcvyan mvo rē-hotvwv cvnaket omēpaten... Mvo asesepvs, cvkihcen, mvo asesehpin, 'svcayet, 'svcayet cvhvpo em vhēckusan resvcohret omet... Racvhvtvpecihcet okat, Heyvn likit cehēcin, vyēpet cehvpo rorehpetsken, vyeparēs. Momis vnhopuetake hokkolet welakēt omēs. Mvn vm vcayēcēt hueretskvrēs, cvkicvntut omen... Okvyat, Este estitut omehaks? kicin... Poset hvmketut omen kowakkuce mvt hvmken ont on okis. Monkv mvn vcayēcet hueretskvrēs, makvntvs.

agile, [the lizard] couldn't do anything... The tiger jumped on the lizard and clawed him, and then jumped halfway up a tree, moving its tail back and forth... Again the tiger would claw it, and then jump back into the tree... The creature that had caught me was being defeated, and the tiger was unaffected and still very agile... He kept on and on until he overcame the thing that had caught me, and I thought, Surely it is tak-ing me to its den, but when the tiger had first begun clawing the lizard, it dropped me and I had lain there without moving while the two fought... Finally the giant lizard that had caught me was defeated, left me there, and slowly disappeared toward its den, and right away the tiger came and stood looking at me: Are you not dead? he asked, but I thought he only meant to do me harm and lay there speechless... If you aren't dead, I'm going to help you. Get up. Get up and sit facing east, he told me... Getting up, I sat facing east as he circled me four times... Now climb upon my back, he said... No, for I am quite heavy, I said to him, but [he said,] It'll be all right. It's my custom to carry stags on my back. So it will be quite all right for me, for this is my way. Go ahead and get on my back, he said, and I got on his back, and he took me back on every path the lizard had brought me on... When we came to where I was first captured, my gun, which had been tossed aside, was lying there. Here is a gun. Could it not be yours? he asked... That is my gun, I replied... Well, then, pick it up, he told me and I picked it up... There was also a shot pouch sitting there... Could this not be yours? he asked... I looked at it and it was mine... Take it, too, he told me, and I picked it up, too, and he took me on and on until we were within sight of my camp... He let me off his back, and then said, I will wait and watch until you reach your camp, and then I will leave. But I have two children. You must protect them for me always, he said to me... Are they human? I asked... One is a cat and the other is a bobcat. So these you will protect, he said.

Moman vrēpit ervlakit omvyvntat, ạrit omvyētvnket fayẹpit arit omvyisan penwvt aohtvmēcet omen... Mvn vyopkēpit, arit ayit erorvyan mv
penwv ohlikat ielecvn naket anekēyen hehcit omvyan, mv nake
okhoyvtēt mvt aret omen hehcit momusen mvn okhoyvtētok kohmit...
Wihket likin vyẹpet mv penwv ohlikan eroret omisat... Momusen mv
penwvn ohtaskat mv penwvt tvmkehpen mvttecihcet ayen hẹre mahen
eraaklvtiken omat... *Oh, Lord*, makacoken... Hiyomof okhoyvtēs, kohmit
oh-ahyet... Vnhessē, ēyvnvttēcetskeko? kicvyan, eturwv-nērkvn
ossicēpet hvlvtēt matan vlicetvn kont omis, estomēceko tayet... 'Sakliket
okēpan ohkin, hvlattehcet, vwihket, letkehpen... Vyẹpvyvntvs, maket
onayesasvntvs, maket onahoyvnts, mahokvnts cē.

So after all this I arrived home, and hunting being my way of life, I was
hunting [one day] when turkeys began flying nearby... I began to creep
toward them, and as I crept forward and got to where the turkey was sitting, I saw something moving beneath it and saw it was one of those I
was told to protect... I stopped my effort and let [the cat] approach the
turkey... He pounced on the turkey, but the turkey flew off and he missed
and finally fell down... Oh, Lord, [the cat] said. This is the time I am to
fulfill the request, I thought, and went over... My friend, have you not
injured yourself? I asked. It had dislodged an eyeball and was trying to
put it back, but could not... As he sat I talked to him, but he jerked it out,
tossed it away, and ran off... I then went away, someone told, it's been
told, it was said.

17

Rabbit tries to straighten riverbeds

The animals have a meeting and decide all the rivers should be made straight. When they try to appoint someone for the task, each refuses except Rabbit. They tell him to take the water flow and not to look back, but before going very far, he looks back, is scared by all the water, and begins running back and forth. The waterways are Rabbit's path.

The shapes of bodies of water are often explained through stories in Creek. In this story, the twisting of waterways is attributed to Rabbit's path. Among Florida Seminoles, the great snake in story 10 is sometimes said to have created the Kissimmee River. This is one of the few stories where Rabbit appears vulnerable.

Nake ponvttv vtēkat nvkaftvtēs. Momet vkerrickv ocēt omakvtēs. Momat hvccet lvpotlvkēt omvrēn eyacaket, mv ohfvccvn esnvkaftet omvtēs. Momēt vpoket vkerrickv hayaket omat mv hvcce lvpotlvkē hakvrē mvn opunvyēcaket esvpokvtēs.

Momen Cufet mvn likvtēs. Mon estit ome tayet os komet mv nvkaftē vpokat em enhonret kihocēto 'stomis, Vcomekot os, makephoyen oman, mv cufe tat, Vnet omvyēs, maket likvtēs. Mont omis em enhonrekot omhoyan, estit omē tayēs kont kihocof, Cufet, Vnet omarēs! makēpvtēs.

Momen estit omē tayēs komhoyē tayat omylkvt respokēpet oman, Cufet, Vnet omarēs! makēpet omen... Momusen mv nvkaftē vpokat este estit omē tayēs komhoyē este em enhonrē esasvtē omylkvn ohmelhohyen, Vcomekot os, makē ylket respokehpen, momusen, Mv cufe, Vnet omarēs makē likan omvkētan os hvmket kihcen... Mvt omētes, maket okakat, Enhonrat okēs. Mvt omvrēs, kihocvtēs. Momen mvn okēpekv, Estomēt omvranen omat vm onvyatskvrēs, maket likēpvtēs. Mon esfullet nake omylkvn em etetahket okakat, Uewv efvkvn hvlahtet esvyetskvrēs. Mont esayetskat, ceyopv rahecekot 'sayet... ēkvnv etewvlvpkēn wvkecetskvrēs, kicet em punayet momehcet... Momusen uewv efvkv tat iesemhohyen momusen esayvtēs.

Mont hvte hopvyē 'svyeko monket, mv eyopv rafulotikē rahecvranekon kicet em punayet okhoyet omētan, mata hvte 'svyeko mahet naket estomet ont omen... Mv este yopv rahecetvt vcakētut omehakes? komet 'saret... Momusen mv eyopv rahēcan, uewv lvokvntot, momēt uewv sēhoneckē omēt... Mv uewv fvkv hvlatat vtēkusen 'saret ohmvtet hēcat, momusen em penkahlet... Mv uewv fvkv lvpotkē 'svyvranvtē momusen em penkahlet... Mv uewv lvokē momvtēkat cvcakken omat, uewvn vcak-elvrēs komat vtēkuset, momusen resletiket eskenahnēcet mata hēckusen

Animals of every kind had a meeting. And they all had one thing in mind. They wanted the rivers to be straight, and for that reason they were meeting. They sat discussing ideas and ways that the rivers might become straight.

Now Rabbit was there. When they tried to appoint someone to do the job, they would all refuse, saying, I am unable, but the rabbit sat saying, I can do it. They had no confidence in him, though, and as they thought of people who could do it and said so, Rabbit kept saying, I'll do it!

Now everyone they felt could do the job had refused, but Rabbit kept saying, I'll do it!... Then when all those in whom the group felt confident had said, I am unable, one of them said, That rabbit who's been saying I'll do it should be considered... Let him do it, they said, He has the desire. He will be the one, they said. And because he meant it, [Rabbit] said, Tell me how it should be done, and sat and waited. They made all the preparations and said, Take hold of the water flow and go forth. And as you go, do not look back behind you... Take it, laying it across the land, they told him, talking with him at length... Then they handed him the water flow and he left right away.

But before going very far with it, [Rabbit thought about how] they had told him he was not to turn and look back, and before going he knew something was not right... Is it so sacred to look back behind yourself? he wondered... Then immediately he turned and looked back, and saw water that looked like flash flooding, and the water was awesome... When he saw he barely held the water flow, right away he became fearful of it... He became fearful of the straight water flow he was going to carry... If that awesome flood catches up with me, I'll drown in the water, he 'saret... Uewv-nene 'tepvkohlusēn hayet ont eraatet okat, Tokvs. Mv nake okatskisē tat hiyomat 'tetaket os, yemaken, vketēcakan, momusen mata hĕckusen 'saret, hvcce 'tepvkohlusēn hayet momēcet aret ohkvten, okakat, Mvn nake momēt omēton okeyat, cēmet ǫketsken, wiketv cehayet omēs, kicet, ehanet vyēcihocvtēt omen... Mvt uewv-nene hayvtēt omistvnts maket okhoyekv, Cufe em vretvt omēs, hvcce lumlohat vtēkat maketvts omvnts cē.

thought, and right away he ran with it in a back-and-forth, winding manner in the distance... He had made little winding waterways and came back, saying, Now. The thing you were concerned about is now complete, and when they checked, right away, only a short distance from where they were, he had made little winding waterways, and they said, We knew how it would be and we said so, but you insisted, so we gave you the job, they said, and they scolded him and sent him away... He was the one who made the waterways, it's said, so they are Rabbit's path, wherever the rivers are, the saying was.

18

Twisted Horn steals man's heart

People gather to plan a dance and discover a man lying asleep. Toad determines that Twisted Horn has taken the man's heart high up above. A mouse volunteers to retrieve the heart, and a spider makes a ladder for him. Twisted Horn keeps human hearts locked in a box, and the mouse gnaws at it. The mouse brings the heart back down and places it back in the man, who wakes up.

A similar story is told among Florida Seminoles (Jumper 1994:69–71). Betty Mae Jumper adds that because of the mouse's heroism, the people pledge not to chase mice away when they eat the corn "hearts" (corn germs) in the fields.

Este sulkēt nvkaftet vpokvtēs. Momen mv momē vpokat opvnkvn hayet vpoket omvtēs. Moman mvn vpohokof, este hvmket nocepēt wakken eshecakvtēs. Mont vketēcaket oman, vhoneceko tayēpet omen, naket estomet omat kerretv kont este tat fullvtēs. Momet este estit estohmen kerrē tayen omat kont vpoket vkerrickv hayakvtēs.

Mont este em enhonret omhoyis, Vcumekut omēs, makephoyen... Ayen, sopaktvn em pohvthoyan, Vnet omarēs, makvtēs. Mont nettv hokkolen vm ehakatskvrēs, makvtēs. Momen mvn okekv, em ehahokvtēs. Mon vrakputokēt nettv hvmkat wakkvtēs. Momis, Naket sepekut omēs, mahket hvtvm hvlwan vhecēt wakkvtēs. Mont mvo nettv hvmken wakkvtēs. Mont okat, Mi hvlwan Yvpe Esfvlvlakvt efēken em esēpet omekv; mvn estit erem ēsen omat, heyv este tat ahesakēs, makvtēs.

Momen hvtvm mvn estit vyē tayat hvtvm hopohoyvtēs. Momen vyēpen este 'menhonret omhoyis omeko vlket vyēpusymmvliken... Cesse-cahtu-cen vtothoyet oman, Vnet omarēs, estit vccakvn hayen omat, makvtēs.

Mohmen hvtvm vccakv-hayvn hopoyet vpohokvtēs. Mon ayen vcokrvn-wvn vtuthoyen mvt vccakv hylwē erorēn hayvtēs.

Mon momusen mvn vccakv tat 'tetakekv momusen mv cesse-cahtucv tat vyēpvtēs, mv Yvpe Esfvlvlakv likat. Mont ayet erem orvtēs. Mont mēcēpet mv Yvpe Esfvlvlakv vcule tat wakkēpen erem orvtēs. Mont tohahvwvn licēt omat mvn este efēke vtehēt omacoket omat 'sem vlikēn omēpen... Momusen mv tohahvwvn enrolvketvn eyahcet, momusen mv tohahvwv tat mv cessuce em vkvlaken, yvpe esfvlvlakv vcule tat pohvtēs. Momet mvn pohat, Cesse enkvnowv soho! maket wakkēpvtēs. Momen mv ces-suce tat vliket mv tohahvwv em vrolakvtēs. Mont em vrolakan, este

Many people once had a meeting. And they were gathered to hold a dance they had planned. While they were sitting there, they found a man lying asleep. After looking him over, they couldn't wake him up, and everyone wanted to know what was wrong. They decided someone should somehow find out what was wrong.

Just when they thought they had found the person who would find out, each one said, I am unable, and so it went on... When they appealed to a toad, he said, I'll do it. Now you must wait for me for two days, he said. They waited, as he had requested. So [Toad] lay face down for one day. But he said, There is nothing there, and then he lay looking way upward. Now he lay there for one day also. Then he said, Way up high Twisted Horn has taken his heart; if someone can go and get the heart, this man will live, he said.

Now once again they looked for someone who might go. All the ones they were sure might go, all were unable, and so it went on and on... The little red mouse was asked, and he said, I'll do it, if someone will make a ladder.

So once again they met to find a ladder maker. And so it was that a spider was asked, and he made a ladder that went up high enough.

So now that the ladder was made, the little red mouse started out to where that Twisted Horn lived. He went until he got there. When he arrived, the old Twisted Horn had in fact done it and was just lying around. He had a box in which he kept human hearts, but it was locked... Right away the mouse wanted to open the box, so he immediately began gnawing at it, and old Twisted Horn heard him. And when he heard him, he said, Mouse in the corner so-ho! as he lay there. But the little red mouse kept on gnawing and finally made a hole in the box. And through the hole [he efēke encvwēpvtē est' efēke pvsvtkēpat sasen, momen hvtvm hvte pvsvtkusekat mvo sasen, hvtvm mv este hvte em ēsat wenakē hēret vpiken eshehcet... Momusen mvn ehset momusen eresvtepvranet okat mv Yvpe Esfvlvlakv tat taṇ 'mvtvhiket momehcet... Momusen mv vccakv kvmhkaken rasaktaskēpvtēs.

Mont esaret resem vlahket mv este wakkate efēke yem pihken, mv este nocē wakkvtē vhonēcvtēs. Mont vhonēcat, okat, Mvtat cvnohcvt tis ca! maken... Cenocat tvlket omeks. Momis Yvpe Esfvlvlakv cefēken cem ehset, hvlwēn 'svyēpet ohmvten... Estohmet estometv vkerricet fullet omeyvnket, vkerrickv pum etetahket estvtohtet ohmēn... Cefēke tat escenhēcet omhoyen ecehonēcet os. Mvt mont omekaten omat, momusen celēpet ont omis: taẏyen cem vnicet omhoyan oketskes, kihocen... Nake momēt momat kẹ̄rrvyesekot hvte cvnocet omatet vcvhonēcet os komvyat tạlkuset okvyis, makesasvtēs, mahokvnts, maket onahoyvnts cē.

could see] human hearts that [Twisted Horn] had taken: there were hearts that had already died, and there were some that were not quite dead, and he found the one recently taken and it was very much alive... Then he took it and was going to bring it back, and he spoke to that Twisted Horn, scolding him severely... Then he went to the ladder and with much noise, carried it down quickly.

He brought it back and placed the heart back into the man who lay sleeping, and the man who lay sleeping woke up. And as he awoke, he said, What a sleep!... You weren't just sleeping, [they said]. Twisted Horn took your heart and had carried it off way up high... We went around wondering what to do and arranged for someone to go... Your heart was found and that is why you woke up. If that hadn't been done, you would have been dead: you've really been helped, they told him... I didn't know, I thought I'd fallen asleep and woken up, that's all I meant, someone once said, it was said, it was told.

19

Old dog saves master from Long Claws

A man goes hunting with his dogs. A little boy comes to the camp every night, saying he's been sent for meat, and he is given some. The fourth night, the old dog warns his master that the boy is not human and that he is after the man. When the boy returns, they flee, but the creature chases them and captures the young dogs one by one. The man and the old dog hide in a hollow log. The creature's claws penetrate the log, but the dog gnaws them off and kills Long Claws.

Here, as in story 4, we see that dogs are keenly aware of danger, and so able to see through witchcraft.

Este enhvmkusēt fakvn ayvtēs. Mont vrēpvtēs. Hofonof fakv vpeyēpat hofonēn fullēt omvtēs.

Monkv mv este ehiwvo sekot omvtēs. Mont arēt omvtet ayet omvtēs. Mon vyēpet enhopvyē 'tetayen eroret momusen ehvpo erhayēpen fayēpat vrēpēt omvtēs. Mont punvttuce tat tayen pvsvtēpēt omēpet onkv, nake hompetv tat ocepē hēret taklikēpēt omvtēs. Momatet efvn sulkēn ēyvpvyēt omvtēs. Mont ayen mv ehvpo hayē erlikate mv tis hofonē haken, naket mv hvyayakē vtēkan aret omacoket omis avtekot omen... Mont os, kont omis mv este taklikvtēs.

Mont ayen em vlakē hakvtēs. Momat cepvnusēt aret omvtet aatet vlaket okat, Vpeswvn rem pohepvs, mahoken arit omis, kicvtēs. Mont mvo vpeswv tat tayēcekv, ēmvtēs. Mon 'svyēpvtēs. Momat hvtvm rennerē hvmke hvtvm ervlakvtēs. Mont okat, mvn maket okvtētok matvpomēn kicet okat, Vpeswvn rem pohepvs, mahoken arit omis, hvtvm yekicen, hvtvm ēmvtēs.

Mont ēmet oman, hvtvm hofonekon hvtvm ervlaket, hvtvm, Vpeswvn rempohepvs mahoken arit omis hvtvm yekicen, hvtvm ehmen esayof, efv vculet totkv pvlhvmkēn atakwakkēpet okat, Mv nake arat este tokot aret oman, estet ont os kont vpeswv ēmēt ontskehaks? kicvtēs. Mon mv estet okat, Estet omat okēt os kont, ēmet omis, kicvtēs. Momen mv efv vculet okat, Vpeswvn cem pohen ēmetsken, ayen vpeswvt cenahen omat, cēmen 'secepvyetvn kont aret oman, kerrekut ēmet ontskes. Monkv mucv hvtvm ervlahket hvtvm vpeswv yecem pohen, ēmetsken omat, momusen 'mete-takvccvs. Mont yv nake cehvpo ocat wihketsken, vpeyvkvrēs. Mont vpēyēn omēto 'stomis, epossēcvrētok, efv mvnettvlket cem vnicvkvrē tis os kicen takkakvtēs.

A man once went hunting alone. And he took his time going about. Long ago those going hunting went for a long time.

Now this man had no wife. And he set out. When he had gone a good distance, he set up camp and began his hunting routine. He killed many small animals, so he stayed in his camp with plenty to eat. The hunter had taken many dogs with him. It had been quite some time since he had made camp, and it came about that every day at daybreak he knew something was wandering nearby but it would not come to the camp... So that's how it is, he thought, and remained in his camp.

As time went on it began to come to the camp. It had been a little boy, and he came up and said, I'm here because they told me to go and ask for some meat. So having all kinds of meat, he gave him some. [The boy] took it and went away. Now he returned the next night. He came and said the same thing as before, saying, I'm here because they told me to ask for meat, and again [the man] gave him some.

After he gave him some, it wasn't long before [the boy] came again, saying, I'm here because they told me to ask for meat, and when he gave him some again and he went off with it, the old dog lying on the other side of the fire said, That thing going around is not human: Are you giving him meat thinking he is human? he asked. Now the man said, He talks like a human, and so thinking, I give it to him. Then the old dog said, He asks for meat, you give it to him, and in time when you are out of meat, he plans to add you [to his meat gathering], but you keep giving it to him unaware. So next time when he comes and asks you for meat again, when you give it to him, you must get ready. You must leave these things in your camp, and we'll go. And even though we're leaving, he'll chase us, but the young dogs will help you, he told him as they sat in camp.

Mon momvranan okētok, hvtvm mv este omē arate ervlakvtēs. Mon mvn kicet okēpvtētok, Vpeswvn rem pohepvs, cvpuset maket oman arit omis, yekicen, hvtvm vpeswv tat ēmvtēs. Mont ehmen 'svyēpan vtē̜kusen vpeyēpvtēs.

Mont vpeyēpat, vpeyēpen momusen mv nake este omē arvtē tat vtēpacoken ont omis, vpeyēpvtēs. Mon vpēyusē monken cakkēpvcoken, momusen, Efv mvnettvlke toyatskat 'mvlumhaks, kihcen momusen 'mvlumhvtēs.

Mont 'mvlumhen, mv nake tat aret ohmvten em vlahkacoken... Momusen 'tohpvlvtiket esfullēpen, vyē̜pen momusen hvmken mv efvn esehpet ohmen... vpvlwusēt ercvkiken vpēyen, hvtvm cakkēpacoken, hvtvm 'Mvlumhaks, kihohcen, hvtvm 'mvlumhvtēs.

Momen mvn momet omēpētok hvtvm em vlahken, hvtvm etohpvlatkat hvtvm efv hvmken esēpen, omylkusekut ercvkiken vpēyvtēs. Mont mvt momvranen mv efv vcule owalet ohkvten mv efv vcule em maketvn esfackvtēs.

Mon vpēyen, mv efv mvnettvlke tat pokēpen, hvmkusē haket ercakkvtēs. Mon vpēyen, hvtvm cakkēpacoken... Hvtvm mv efv hvmkusate, momusen toskọmēskon esmonkehpen vhoyen... Hvtvm momusen cakkēpacoken oman... Eto-hvoke tis wakket omvnts, 'to-hvoke rakkē tis wakkvnts. Momēt wakken erorhoyet omen mv efv vculet okat, Mv eto-hvokan ecēyvs! mv epucasen kican vtē̜kusen mv este tat mv eto-hvoke ecēyvtēs. Mohmen mv efv vculet yopvn acēyvtēs. Mont mv este, Nake

And as he said it would happen, again the human-like thing came back. And as before, he came and said, I'm here because my grandmother said to go and ask for meat, and again he gave [the boy] meat. And as soon as he gave it to him and [the boy] went off with it, they left.

And as they were going, it was evident that the human-like thing was coming after them, but they kept going. As they were going, it seemed the thing was catching up with them, so [the old dog] said, You young dogs lie in wait, and they lay waiting.

As they lay there, they realized it had been that thing going about, and it had evidently caught up with them... Then they fell upon each other for a long while, and after the thing caught one of the dogs, only a few of the others caught up with them as they went on, but again the thing had evidently caught up with them, and the young dogs were told, Lie in wait! and again they lay waiting.

Once again it came, again they fell upon each other, again it caught one dog, and the few remaining dogs caught up with [the man and the old dog], and they kept going. The events the old dog had prophesied would happen were fulfilled as he had said.

They continued on, all the young dogs having gone, and only one [young dog] remained and caught up with them. As they were going again, the thing had evidently caught up with them... Again the one [remaining young] dog disappeared and did not return, and two continued on... Again the thing had evidently caught up with them... Sometimes there would be a hollow log lying around, a big, hollow log lying around. They came upon one lying there and the old dog said, Get in the hollow log! and as soon

makekot wakkępetskvrēs, mv efv vculet kicētok, nak makekot
wakkvtēs.

Mv nake aassēcē arvtē tat vlahket momusen mv eto-hvoken mv este tat
yecēyet omat kērrat momusen 'mvsekēyet, 'mvkorret ont omis mv hvte
mv nake vlvkeko monkē mv eto cēhoyof, mv efv vculet mv eto-hvoke
cēhohyof mv efv vculet mv eto-hvoke momusen eteyoficvtēs. Mont eto
hvokeko omēn hayet omen kaket ont omis, mv nake arat mvn cēhoyet
mvn wakhokan kērret omet momusen 'mvwosvtēs. Mont mv eto-hvoke
vyofihocat momēn momēcet omhoyat mv nake kerrepētut omekv,
vwicēceko tayet... Mvn 'mvwosat vliket omat, mv momē 'mvwosat
enkusosuwv erfvnvnicē haket omis, mv efv vculet vhomvn liket onkv,
mv enkusosuwv erfvnvnicof iem vwocotket mv efv vculet eslikēpet, mv
nake enkusosuwv enkecētkē poyepvrąnusen hvyvtiken...

Momusen mv nake arat hocefkv tat Enkusosup-Cvpko maketvt aret ont
omis, mv efv vculet mv nake enkusosuwvn em poyēpen hvyatken mv
nake momusen mv efv vculet em osiyet, ehset, elēcvtēs. Moman mv
naket aret omen mv efv vculet elehcet mv este hesayēcvtēs. Mon tokvs,
aossvs ca! Elēcit omis, kicen, aossvtēs. Moman elēcēpet ohkvten
hēcvtēs.

Momen hvtvm ehvpo tatē yefulhokvtēs. Nake estomosis ocusēt omvtētis
wihken pefatket omvtētok, mvn ercvwepetvn eyahcet ohmen yefulhokvtēs. Mont welaket mv ehvpo hayē kakvtē erorhoyvtēs. Mont erorhoyet
okat, mv efv vculet okat, Estvn estomēcēt 'saret omvtē enhecvkēs, kicet
omis, mv este tat penkvlēpētut omis, Mucv tat mv nake omat vwolat
sekot omis os, kicet omen... Mon omat rahēcvkētis okis, kihcet, vcak-
ayvtēs.

as he said this to the master, the man went into the hollow log. Then the old dog went in right behind him. The old dog told the man, You must lie here without saying a thing, and he lay there without saying anything.

The thing that was chasing them came and right away he knew that the man had gotten in the hollow tree, and he poked and dug, but before the thing had come, when the two were going in, as soon as the old dog went in, the old dog closed up the hollow log. He made the tree so that it was not open and they sat waiting, but the thing knew they had hidden in the log and were in there, and began to dig at it. [The] thing knew that the hollow log had been made to close up, so he wouldn't stop... He kept digging and dug until his claws were sticking through, but the old dog sat in front and when the claws were sticking through, he would chew off the ends, so the thing's claws were almost chewed off by daylight...

That thing going about had been called Long Claws, but the old dog had worn down the thing's claws and at dawn, the old dog came out of the hollow log, attacked him, and killed him. So it was that the old dog killed the thing and saved the man's life. All right, now, come on out! I killed him, he said, and [the man] came out. He saw that [the dog] had indeed killed it.

So they returned again to what had been their camp. He had had posses-sions but had left them and run, so they went back wanting to get them. They got back to where they used to camp. When they reached it, the old dog said, Let's go and see what he's done with all that you gave him, but the man was afraid and [the dog] said, Now there isn't anything like that nearby... Well, then, we can go and see, [the man] said, and went with him.

Mon mv vlakvtē fvccvn vhoyan (mv vpeswv vpes-pvkvfken ēmet omvtēs). Moman mv, mv vpeswv pvkvfkē iesēmvtē emonkusen, 'sayē monkvtēs omvtēs komvken erescakcvhēcet vrępet omvten hecakvtēs.*

Mont welaket momusen fayē vretv komē arvtē mvn vtękusen em vhopvniken, momusen mv naket efvo em poyēpet omen, mv efv vcule hvmkuset em vhosken 'svrępet encuko hakusat resvlahket... Mont mv em vnakuecvlke momēn aret omat onayet likesasvtēs, mahokvnts cē.

So they went in the direction the thing had always come from (he had given the thing meat speared on a stick). They saw that he had taken the speared meat he had been given each time and stuck it in the ground.

As they went about, the hunter realized that his hunting trip was ruined, that the thing had done away with all his dogs, and that he only had the old dog left as they returned home... And he told of his experience to those closest to him, it was said.

* The sequence *monkvtēs omvtēs* here should probably be *monkvtēs*.

20
Doe killed by hunter, becomes his wife

A woman and a little child come and stay with a hunter. She reveals that she is a doe that was killed on an earlier trip and warns him not to tell the others how he got her. When they return home, he keeps the secret. After a long time, he decides it would be all right to tell, but when he begins to tell, the woman and her child bound off.

When the man tells the truth, he is rewarded with a wife and child. When he breaks his vow, he loses everything.

Este hvmket fakvn ayvtēs. Mont mv em pvlse sekotat omvtēs. Mont omat enhomvn fakvn aret omat, eco-ecken elēcet omat, vwikvtēs. Momvtēt omvtētan mv ēkvnv em vnakvn fayat ertaklikvtēs. Mont fayēpat vrēpēt omvtēs. Mont nake elēcē hẹrēt estet omēpvtēs. Mont eco tis, monkat nake erem ētv ponvttv sasat, pvsvtēpet taklikẹpvtēs.

Mont arvtē, mvtis hofonē hakēpet oman, vkerricet, Yefulkepvyē tayē ont os, kont omis, hvte taklikē monkof, hoktē, echuswv ocēt resoret omat em enherē hẹret, estaklikēpet omen, mv este honvnwvo matvpomēn omēpen, takkakēpet omvtēs.

Momen mv hoktēt okat, Estomēn hoktē cenhēcket omehaks? cekihocvrēs. Momis estomēn cenhēcket omat, estofvn estin em onvyetskekarēs, kicet, em vsēhvtēs. Mont omen mimv tat, hvte eresvteko monkof, momēn kicet em vsẹhet momēcvtēs. Momen mv hvte momē kicekof okat, Eco-ecke 'lēcet, vwiketskvtēsekot omehaks? kicen, Momēcvyvtēt os, kicen, Vnet mv eco-ecke elehcē vwiketskvtē toyis. Mont omet cekērrit omis. Mv omēcicēn, iesecoh-atet omis. Monkv cencuko yefulkēpetskat 'sepoyetskē tayen omat, mvn pokicvs kont omis, kicen... 'Seceyvkarēs, kicvtēs. Momen, momusen ehiwv hakẹpet estaklikẹpet omvtēs. Mont hoktē matat cvfeknēt, nake ocē mvtat lopịcusēt omẹpen, mv este honvnwvo orēn encakē haket, 'saret resvtēpvtēs.

Mont 'svrēpet resvlvkēpvtēs. Momen momē fakvn aren hoktē enhēcket omvtēs. Monkv mv hoktē estomēt enhēcket omvtē em pohohēto 'stomis, estofvn onvyeko tạyusēt omvtēs. Mont kakẹpet omvtētan, hofonē hakẹpet oman, kakẹpet oman, mv hoktē estomēt enhēcket omvtē kerretv komat

A man went hunting. And he had no wife. Previously he had gone hunting, killed a mother doe, and thrown her away.* And so it was that he set up camp near the place he had hunted the time before. And he went about hunting. And he was a very good hunter. And he killed deer or other wild animals in the area and continued camping.

He had been out for quite a long time and began to think, I ought to go home, but while he was still at his camp, a woman with a little child came, and being very attracted to him, she stayed on with her child, and the man felt likewise and they stayed together.

Then the woman told him, They will ask you, How did you get a woman? But you must never tell how you got her, you must never ever tell anyone, she warned him. And before he had started back from there, she warned him again. But before she warned him, she asked him, Have you never killed a mother doe and thrown her away? I have, he said... I am the mother doe you killed and threw away. That is how I knew you. That is the reason I came to you with my child. So when you return home, I need to know if you'll take us with you, she said... I'll take you, he said. It was then that she became his wife while they were still camped. And this same woman was able-bodied and could do things, and was nice, and the man really loved her, too, and brought her back. And he finally returned home with them.

So it was that he found this woman while on a hunting trip. Even though he was asked how he got the woman, he never told. So they lived together, and after a while, where they lived, there were those who wanted to know where he got his wife and would ask. Now the man was

* The word *vwikvtēs* means 'threw her away', but the same word appears in stories 24 and 25, and may be a fixed expression meaning '(kill and) bring down or fell (a deer)'.

este em pohakat svsēt omvtēs. Momen mv este momēn laksē tayē onkot omvtēs. Momis mv hoktē nake em vsēhat vcak-vyēn onvyeko tayet omvtētok.

Momen hvtvm, hofonē herē hakē 'svpvkētut omen, mv omēcicen, Onay-vyis, estonkis omēs. Mv momē momen hokteu yvwoskē haket omis onkv komet vkerricvtēs. Momof mv hoktē, vcen hocet arvtēs. Mon arof, mv este honvnwv tat, Momusen mv hoktē estomēn vnhēcken omvtē onayvyis. Estonkis omēs, kohmet, hvte onvyetv vlicēcet esliken, mv hoktē vce hocē arvtē iem apohicet huervtet... Momusen kecvpe tat vwihket, ecot omēpvtet, hvce hatken ohcakhēcet ayen, mv echuswvo matvpon vhoyēpvtēs, mahokvnts cē.

not one to lie like that. But he followed the woman's warning and would not tell anyone.

Then it had also been a very long time, and for that reason he thought, I can tell now, it won't matter. The woman is used to being here, he thought to himself. Now the woman was busy pounding corn. As she worked, the man thought, Now I can tell how I got the woman; it will be all right, he thought, and just as he had sat down and begun to tell, the woman pounding the corn stood listening... Instantly she threw the pounder down, and being a deer, she took off with her white tail sticking up, and with her child, too, they went in the same way, it was told long ago.

21
Buzzard doctors Rabbit

Bear and Rabbit are friends. Rabbit visits Bear, who tells his wife to cook some food. Needing grease, Bear cuts around his stomach and produces enough for the beans. Bear then visits Rabbit, who tells his wife to cook some beans. Needing grease, Rabbit cuts around his stomach, but punctures it. Bear hires Buzzard to be the doctor, and Buzzard instructs them to place Rabbit in a house with food and an opening at the top. They hear Rabbit making noises inside, but Buzzard says it is only the doctoring. Buzzard eats Rabbit, leaves the bones in a heap, and escapes through the opening (cf. Swanton 1929, Creek story 61).

This is a well-known story. Where Rabbit is often cunning, here, as in story 17, his overconfidence gets him in trouble.

Nokoset, momet Cufe 'tepakat, etenhēssvtēs. Mont ehisakvtēs. Mont empvlse ocvkē hahkof, Cufet liken Nokoset hēcvtēs. Mont hēcet omet, Vnhessē! Naken estont momēt liketska? kicen, Fēkapet likit omis cē, kicvtēs. Mont Nokoset okat, Rvncuko-pericvs! kicvtēs. Mont, Erorarēs, maket Cufe tat likvtēs. Mon vyēpvtēs, Nokose tat.

Mont enliketv eroret Nokose tat liken, Cufe tat vrēpvtet erem orvtēs. Mont liket omen 'tem punahoyet kakēpvten, momusen Nokose tat Hompetvn hayvs! ehiwvn kicvtēs. Mont Nokoset okvtēs. Momusen mvn okhoyekv, Nokose ehiwv tat momusen hompetv-hakv vlicēcet aret omat, Nehat sepekot oman os cē, ehiwvt Nokosen kicvtēs. Moman hvtēc, maket, Nokose tat aret, eslafkvo eraehset, 'mvkaskvsēcet aret ayat, neha herakusēn resvlakvtēs.

Momat mv eslafkv esē ayat hvteceskv ele mahen 'mvlaffan, neha sepekon... Hvtvm envrke mahen hvtvm 'mvsatan, mvn neha heraket ocvten mvo ra cawvtēs. Mont okat, Heyvn oces, ehiwvn kihcet iemvtēs. Mon mvn okētok momusen ennorihohcen, mont tvlakon 'sem ensiho-hyen tayē hēren hompakvtēs.

Mont kakēpvten, momusen Cufe tat ervtepvranet omet momusen matvpomēn estekicvtēs. Cēmeu ervm orepetskvrēs, maket omen... Momvrēs, kicvtēs.

Momen mvn okvtētok, Nokose tat ayvtēs. Cufen encuko-pericvranet ayet omvtēs. Mont aret erem oret omen, 'tem punahoyet kakēpvtēs. Mon ayen Cufe tat, ehiwvn okat, Tvlakon punnoricvs. Hompetv punhayvs, maket liken, momusen Cufe 'hiwv tat, momusen hompetv-hakv vlicēcet aret omat, nehat sepekon, Cufen yem onayet okat, Nehat sepekan os, kihocen aret... Momusen eslafkvn eraehset ayat elen 'mvsatan naket sepekon,

Bear and Rabbit became friends. And they both took wives. Now after each had gotten a wife, Bear saw Rabbit just sitting around. Upon seeing him, he said, My friend! Why are you sitting there? I am just sitting here resting, [Rabbit] told him. Then Bear said, Come and visit me! I will come over, said Rabbit as he sat. So Bear went on his way.

Bear returned to his home and was sitting around, and Rabbit got there after some time. Now they sat and talked a long while, and then Bear told his wife, Cook some food! Now it was Bear who said it. And because he meant it, Bear's wife immediately began the cooking, [but,] There's no grease, Bear's wife told him. Well, then, wait, he said, and Bear got a knife, filed it, and went and returned with nice pieces of fat.

Now the first time he left carrying the knife, he tried slicing around his ankles but there was no fat, so again he tried cutting around his stomach, found good fat, and took some. So he said to his wife, Here's some, and handed it to her. Just as he had said, the food was cooked, the beans were well seasoned, and they ate hungrily.

Afterward as they sat around, Rabbit was preparing to leave and said likewise: You, too, come to my place, he said [to Bear]... I will, he answered.

And as he had promised, Bear went. He went just to visit Rabbit. Now when he got to where he lived, they sat and talked. And after a while, Rabbit told his wife, Cook us some beans. Make us some food, he said as he sat, and then Rabbit's wife started cooking, but there was no grease, and she came and told Rabbit, There's no grease... Then Rabbit got a knife and scraped his foot, but there was nothing, and again he tried cutting hvtvm nvrke ma̧hen laffan nvrke 'sohrolvkēt, lvfiyet, Towēk! Towēk! makacoken... Nokoset pohhet ayet eroran, nvrken 'sohrolvkēpet, likētt okēpen... Kut, vnhessē! Ta̧yen ēyvhopvnetskeko? Vntat omvyvnkan ontsket ont os, kicet omis, 'sohrolvkēpet hoyvnēpekv, momusen Nokose tat vlēkcv hopoyat arvtēs. Momet Sulen vtotvtēs. Mon mv vlekcvranat okat, Afke-rakkon hayen aswvkechoyen em vlēkcet omvyvnts. Mont cuko ofvn wakket omvranēt os. Mon hvtvm cuko onvpvt ohrolvkēt omvranet os, makvtēs.

Momen mv nake estomēt omvranēs makē vtēkat em metetakvtēs. Mohmet mv cuko ofv makat mvo omy̧lkvn 'metetakuehocvtēs. Momen okat, Osiyit, fulotkit, arit hy̧lwēn vyēpvyof, rahēcet omhoyvnts, makvtēs.

Mont mv cufe ē-enokkicat mv cuko ofv rienwvkechoyvtēs. Mon mv sule tat momusen encēyvtēs. Momet hofonē haken, Cufet, Towēk, maken... Estomētsken oka? kihocof... Hiyan nake 'sem ocvyan ennokkētut oks, maken, wihoken oman, hvtvm hofonē haken hvtvm maken... Eston oka? kihocan... Mvn afken 'mvtenkēn oks, maket papet esliket, omy̧lkvn lokehpet fune ty̧lkusēn toheksihcet... Momusen osiyet, fulotket aret sumkehpen, rahechoyan fune ty̧lkusen, toheksican hechoyvtēs, mahokvnts cē.

around his stomach, but punctured and cut it: Tweek! Tweek! they heard him say... Bear heard it and went to see and saw Rabbit sitting there with a punctured stomach... Oh, my friend! Have you damaged yourself? I can do it, but you shouldn't have, he said, but because he had already punctured himself, Bear went to look for a doctor. Now he hired a buzzard. And [the buzzard] who was to doctor him said, Make lots of mush and set it nearby: that's how I always doctor. And [Rabbit] has to lie in the house. And then the roof of the house should have an opening, he said.

And each request that he made was fulfilled. They got the room prepared as he had requested. Then [Buzzard] said, When I go out, circle around, and go high up in the sky, someone can go see about him: that's the way it's done, he said.

So they laid the rabbit who had injured himself in the house for [the buzzard]. Immediately the buzzard went in to him. After a long time, they heard Rabbit saying, Tweek... What are you doing to him? they would ask... When I apply heat, it hurts him, he said, so they waited, and after a long time, he would make the sound again... Why is he making that sound? they asked... I'm stuffing him with the mush, he said as he sat eating [Rabbit], and he ate him up and left only the bones in a heap... Then he went out, circled around, and disappeared, and when they went to check, they found only bones in a heap, it was said.

22
Cow wants a knife

Cow wants to own a knife and asks God for one. God says she must stay in the cabbage patch all night, but she eats up all the cabbage. Then she says she only gives birth to one calf at a time, but wants to give birth to many. Having failed the test, she is told she will not have a knife and will only give birth to one calf, that her mouth and stomach are already large enough (cf. Swanton 1929, Creek story 80).

Wakvt eslafkvn ocēt ometvn eyacet omet Hesaketvmesē em pohvtēs. Mont okat, Hesaketvmesē! kicen, Nak 'stoma? kihocen okat, Eslafkvn ocvyēt ometvn cvyacet okis, kicen... Mon omat vsin, esse-taphot eslikēs. Mvn aretsken hvyatken omat, mvn eslafkv tat cemarēs, kihcen... Momusen mvn eslafkv eyacēpet aret okēpekv, momusen mv momē eslafkv epoyetv komat, momusen mv esse-tapho eslikat ohcehyet aren hvyatkvtēs.

Momat mv esse-tapho ocēn mv wakv ohcēyet omvtētat mv esse-tapho ocvtē omylkvn lokēpet mv nerē hymkusat... Ohhvyatken mv wakv ervlaket omen moman hvtvm, Hvmkusēn sicvyēt ont omekv, mvo sulken kayvyē tayet ometvn cvyac makē 'svpaket ont mvn esse-tapho ohpiket omhoyvtēs. Mont omen mvn eskerretv komat okhoyet omat mvn kerrekot mv esse-tapho omylkvn lokēpet omen okatet, Eslafkvo ocekot mont wakuce hvmkusēn sicēt ometskvrēs. Sulkēn sicēt ometvn ceyaceto 'stomis, cenvrke rohhvtvlaket omekis tayēpēs. Momet eslafkvo ocekot cecokwv ocetskat tylkosis cem etetayēpet onkv, naken remontvlē ceyaceko tayat oketskes, kicet... Mv nake eyacē makat em momēceko vlket omvtēs, maket okhoyvnts, maket onahoyvnts cē.

Cow wanted to own a knife and asked the Lord. Lord! she said, What's the matter? she was asked, I want to own a knife, she said... Well, then, over there is a cabbage patch. If you can stay there till morning, I'll give you the knife, he said... She wanted the knife very badly, so in order to get the knife, she wandered around in the cabbage patch till morning.

When the cow went into the cabbage patch, there had been cabbage, but in just one night she ate up all the cabbage that was there... The cow returned when morning came and said, I give birth to only one calf and I want to have many, and this added request was the reason she had been put in the cabbage patch. This had been a test, but she didn't know that and had eaten all the cabbage, so she was told, You will not have a knife and will give birth to only one calf. You want to have many calves, but your stomach doesn't need to be larger, it's large enough. And the mouth you have is enough for you without a knife, so you don't need anything more, he told her... The things she had requested he did not grant, it was said, it was told.

23

Hunter captured by eagle

A hunter is captured by a giant eagle and taken to its nest. The eagle returns with a bear, and the man roasts it and feeds it to the eaglets. With time, the eaglets grow bigger and the man tames them, flying on their backs. One day he takes one out, hits it on the head to make it land, and escapes.

This story (the "Roc" motif) is also told among Florida Seminoles, Alabamas, and Cherokees (Lankford 1987:74–76; Jumper 1994:45–47;). Betty Mae Jumper notes that the eagle does not have the same importance in the Southeast as it does among western tribes.

Este hvmket... Fayēpet aret omatet, fēkapit likvyof, hvsen naket em vrv-
nayet omen, hēcvyan, lvmhe-rakkot aret omehpvtet, mv fēkapvyē likvyat
vlahket cvsēpvntos. Momat naken vnnokkicekot 'svcvyēpet... Mimv
hvlwē on vtēpet, vrēpet omehpvtet eresvcorvntos, makesasvtēs,
mahokvnts.

Mont omat mimv hvlwat lvmhuce vpoyepēt omet ohmvtet mvn resv-
corvntvs. Mont momusen lvmhucet cvlokvkvranet omat tvlkēs
komvken... Rehcvwihket mv lvmhe-rakko sumkēpet ohmat, nokosen
elēcēt resvlakvntvs. Momusen mv nokose tat torofehpit, hotopehpit
hompēpit, momet lvmhucvlkeu hompaken hompeyvntos.

Momet mv lvmhucvlkeu etohkvlkēt vpoket omen, mv lvmhe tat naken
komat, mvo eco tis elēcet resvlaken, mvo hotopēpit, hompēpit likit
omvyētvnkan... Mv lvmhuce vculvkēpat fulletv yekcicē fullē haket omen,
momusen mv lvmhucvlke 'sahkopvnēpit yvmvsąkusē hayēpit omit...
Momēcarēs komit omit, mv lvmhucvlke ohlikēpit estomusat esarit rasfu-
lotkvyē haket omet... Mucvt on omat vyeparēs, komit omit, estomēt omē
tayat vkerrickv vm etetaket omat... Mv lvmhe vculat fayetv ayat yafkē-
ylken rvlaket ont omen... Mvn momusen lvmhe tat fayvranat vyehpen—
momusen lvmhuce tat vculvkēttt, momusen rakrvkē hērē haket omet,
fulletvo naket 'sem estonko hakvkēt omekv—momusen ohlikit 'sayvyat
hopvyē tis resfulotkit resvlakvyē haket omētvnket... Hvtvm 'sayvyat mvn
momēcvyēt omen mvn eskerricvyēt omet omet omētvnket,* momusen
Matan cvmomēcvranet omēs, kont omētok, tąn 'svcayet omen, momusen
'svcayet omen momusen 'sayit omvyisat 'svcvhopvyēcē haken... Momusen
ekvn ennvfikin mahyomecihcin omētok, escvfulotkat escvkvncvpuecet
ayet omen 'sayin... Rem vhlvpatkat omētok mi hvlwat ētan yescvfulketv

* The Creek *mvn eskerricvyēt omet omet omētvnket* should probably be *mvn eskerricvyēt omet
omētvnket.*

A man [once said]... I had been out hunting and when I sat down to rest,
something obscured the sun, and as I looked, I saw that it had been a
large eagle, and he came to where I sat resting and caught hold of me. As
he carried me along, he did not hurt me at all... He had come from very
far up and took me there, someone once said, it was said.

Now way up high the eagle had a nest of baby eagles and took me there.
At the time I thought to myself that the little eagles were going to eat me
up... The eagle left me there and disappeared, and returned with a bear it
had killed. Right away I skinned the bear, roasted it, and ate it, and the
little eagles ate, too, and we all ate.

So it was that we all lived together, the little eagles and I, and the eagle
would go out and bring back whatever it wanted, sometimes a deer it had
killed, and I would roast these, too, and eat while living there... The little
eagles were getting older and going about getting stronger, and I began to
play with the little eagles and made them very tame... And as I had plans,
I would get on the little eagles and go out a short distance, turn around,
and come back... This time I'm going to leave, I thought, so I made my
plans on how to do it... The old eagle would go hunting and return in the
evening every day... So the eagle went to hunt—the little eagles had gotten older and had grown pretty big and traveling was no problem for
them—so I would get on [an eagle] and ride far out and return... Again I
took [a baby] eagle, the same as I usually did, and the eagle, thinking this
was the same as usual, took me, but he kept going and I let him keep
going until we were quite a way off... Then I hit him on the head and
made him dizzy, and he went in a circle as I took him lower and lower...
When his head began to clear and he wanted to take me back up high, I

eyacof, hvtvm ekvn ennvfikin, hvtvm escvfulotket escvkvncvpuecet 'svcayet ēkvnv resvcvlakvntos, makesasvtēs. Mont okat, Mimv hvlwat cefahlē-rakkot yata ēkvnv ocakat ētvpomusēt ocvkepēt omvnts, make-sasvtēs, mahokvnts cē.

would hit him on the head again and he would go in circles again and begin to go lower until he had me back down on the ground, someone once said. Way up high there are big mountains just like we have here, someone said, it was said.

24

Whistling man helps hunter

A man is so unsuccessful at hunting that his family has to boil and eat his leggings. He tries again to hunt and hears a whistling man crossing the treetops. The whistler breaks the man's bow and arrows and returns with new ones. He instructs the man to kill the fourth deer that he sees. The man does so, and is able to kill vast quantities of deer, but doesn't know how to prepare the meat. The whistler returns and shows him. The man is told to show the meat to his mother-in-law, who unwraps it and is knocked against the wall.

This story plays on the antagonism between a man and his mother-in-law.

Este hvmket likvyvntvs, makesasvtēs, mahokvnts. Mont ehiwvo ocēt omet, hopuetakuceu ocēt omet, enhoktvlwvo ocēt omet omat...

Fayvyēto estomis naken elēcvko tayet omēpet omen, likvyvntvs. Momēt omētvnkan, hopuetaket elvwaket omen... Hvf-vtēhkv ocvyēt omētvnkan mv naken enhoret omhoyen omvtēs. Naketut estakliket omen, mv hopue-taket ak-vpohoket omen... Naket omen omat, iem ak-esaks, makit omin... Okatet, Kos, naken puetake em elēcet okēs cē! Iem ak-esaks! cvkihocet omisat iem ak-ēset omat, mv hvf-vtēhkv-leskv ocvyvtēn enhorēpet omehpvtet... Iem ak-eshoyen pvpaken hēcit taklikvyisat momusen ayvyvntvs.

Naken elehcvkotut omat kērrit omvyis, fayvrant ayat, ayet arit cvhvpo erhayēpit eraklikvyvntvs. Momat fotkusēt vrēpesasacoken pohit takwakkēpvyvntvs. Moman eccv-kotaksen cvwēpus ayet arit omvyvntvs. Mont mv eccv-kotakseu atak-vpoyēpit takwakkit omvyisan, mv este fotkē arvcokē pohvyat hvyatkē pokan eton etohtvlkuset yoh-vyēpet oken hēcvyvntvs. Momet vyēpet rvsumiken takwakkvyof, hvtvm erhvtapket ervlakvntvs.

Momat mv eccv-kotakse momet rē 'svpvkēn ocit omvyisekv, momusen mv este vlakat mv rē ocvyan rascahwet, momusen 'mvlvpotē hayet rē tat omv̲lkvn 'svm etekvcēyet 'svm vpvlatet pohyet, momusen hvtvm eccv-kotakseu ratak-ehset mvo kotaticet vyēcicē monket mvo vm etekahcet vm vwihket... Eccv-kotakse rē omakat estomēckv-tokon esaret ontsken ohmvttis, maket takhuerisat vyēpvntvs. Mohmet sumkehpat, hvtvm

There once lived a man, someone once said, it was said. And this man had a wife, had children, and had a mother-in-law, too...

I would go hunting but couldn't kill anything during this time and lived like this. So it was that the children were hungry... I had a pair of leg-gings, and it was those [my wife] was boiling over the fire. Whatever it was, it was sitting down there [cooking] and the children wanted some of it... Whatever it is, get it out for them, I said... Oh, he has killed some-thing for his children! Get it out for them! [my mother-in-law] said, so they took it out for them and I realized [my wife] had been boiling the old leggings I used to have.* She took it out for them, and I sat and watched them eat it awhile, and then left.

I knew that I couldn't kill anything, but I went to hunt, went a distance, set up my camp, and settled in. And I heard someone whistling as I lay there. And I had taken my bow and arrows with me. And I had my bow and arrows lying beside me as I lay there, when I heard that person whistling at daybreak and saw him pass by going tree to tree. Then he kept going till he was out of sight, and when I lay down again, he climbed down and came back.

And I had my bow and arrows, so the man who had come went to where my arrows were and got them, checked to see if they were straight, and broke them all in two, and after throwing them all away, went and got the bow and continued bending it back and forth until he broke that, too, and threw it away... The bow and arrows you carry are worthless, he said, and stood awhile, then went away. Then he went out of sight, but I heard him

* The reference here is sometimes unclear. From the ending of the story, it seems the wife must have been boiling the leggings and the mother-in-law must have been making the sarcastic comments.

fotkat vrēpacoket omisat, hvtvm matvpomēt eto etohtvlkusēt yoh-vyēpet oken hēcit taklikin, ayet rvsumiken... Vcewē haken, hvtvm erhvtvpkēpēs komvken rvlakvntvs. Moman mv fotkē hvte eto yoh-ayof hēcvyan, eccv-kotakse cvwēt yoh-vyēpet oken hēcvyēt omvntvs.

Momen mv erhvtapkē rvlakat eccv-kotakse cawet momet reu 'svpvkēn resvm vlakvntvs. Mohmet okat, Heyvn esfayetskvrēs. Mont estv fvccvn vyvranvyat, vm onahyet okat, Pvne 'svhokkolē erakhvtapketsken, eco rakkēt 'co-honvnwvt vlaken hecetskvrēs. Momis mv tat elehcetskvs. Momen hvtvm vlvkvrēs. Momis mvo elehcetskvs. Momis eco yicē 'sostan cu̜tkosēt vlvkvrēs. Mvn elēcetskvrēs. Mvn elēcofvt, erenyopvn estomvkēn eco elēcepetv ceyacat, mvn estomusēn ceyacat pvsvtepetskvrēs, cvkihcet vyēpet omvnken, momusen mvn okhoyvtētok, momusen ayvyvntvs.

Mont mvn okhoyvnkekv, komvken ayit, mv pvne okhoyvtē erorvyan, momvranen okēpvten eco honvnwv vculet orēn rakkēt vlaket omis, Mv tat elehcetskvs, mahoket omvnkekv, elēcetv 'yackv cvlēpuset omis, monkon cvkihocen arvyet omis onkv komvken likin hoyahnet aret vyeh-pen... Hvtvm likvyof, hvtvm matvpǫmvtēket vlaket omis, Eco yicē esostan cu̜tkuset vlvkvrēs. Mvn elēcetskvrēs! cvkicet okhoyen arvyet omekv, em ehaket likin... Mv eco yicē esostat cu̜tkusē vlvkvranē mahokvtē momepvranen okēpvten, momusen mv eco cu̜tkusat vm vlaken, momusen rahhit, resvwihket likvyof, momusen yicepvranen okephoyvten... Yicaken, pvsatit, pvsatit, pvsatit, pvsatit momehcit, mv pvne fackē ont, hatkē omen hahyit... Momusen Tḁyis omēs, komvken arit omvyisat, momusen vteloyēpit, omy̜lkvn vteloyehpit, hvtvm torofit, vfēsit omvyis, mvo eco vfe-setv tis cvkerrepeko ont 'sak-arvyof... Momusen hvtvm mv este eccv-kotakse vm vpalvtē arē hēcvyvtē hvtvm mvn eroret okat, Eco celayetv tis

whistling again, and I sat and watched him pass by going from tree to tree in the same way as before, and he kept going until he was out of sight. After a long while, he climbed down and came back. When I saw that whistler going across the trees, I saw that he carried a bow and some arrows as he passed by.

When he had gotten down as he returned again, he was carrying the bow and the arrows together and brought them to me. Then he said, You will hunt with these, and told me what direction to go in, saying, You will go down into the second ravine, and there you will see a very large deer, a buck, coming [toward you]. But you must not kill that one. And another one will come. But you must not kill that one, either. But the fourth deer that comes will be a small one. That one, you will kill. When you kill that one, from then on, you may kill whatever kind of deer you want, he told me and went away, and as soon as he told me, I went.

And I thought about what was said to me, and went until I reached the ravine spoken of, and as I was told, a very large old buck was coming, but as I was told not to kill that one, even though I was dying to kill it, because I was told not to, I sat until the buck went past and continued going... When I sat down again, one about the size of the first one came along, but I'd been told, The fourth deer that comes will be a small deer. Kill that one! so I sat and waited... The fourth deer to come would be small, he had said, and sure enough, the small deer came, and right away I shot it, brought it down, and as I was sitting there, they began to come as it had been said they would... And as they came I killed, and killed, and killed, and killed, and when I had finished, the ravine looked almost full, I had made the ravine look white... Then I thought, This ought to be enough, and started gathering them, and gathering them all, I dressed and skinned them, but I didn't even know how to skin the deer as I was wandering

cekẹrresekot ometsken omeko? cvkicen... Cvmomēt omēs. Eco tis elēcvyē onkot omēpet onkv, eco celayetv tis, momet torofetv, vfesetv cvkerrekot omēpēs, kicin... Huerisat momusen aatet, vlahket mv eco lumhat vlahket... Hvtehtvs! mahket, vm vfēset avm pvlatet momehcet... Tokvs. Vcayēcepvs, cvkihcet vyehpen, momusen vcayēcēpit vrẹpit omin... Momusen, Estofvn komat vyepetskvrēs, cvkihcet vyehpen... Momusen eco-vpeswv tat vcayēcēpit omvyis, taklikit omvyvnket, vyehpvyētat omis, puetake tis elvwakēton, vnhomechoyēn arit omvyvnkan omēkv komit omit... Momusen em etetaketvn komit omit, mv eco-vpeswv vteloyēpit omvyisis... Estomehcit vpeswv omvlehcit 'svyvko tayet wvnvyē poyit omvyis, sụlkēt omēpekv, estvmạhet vteloyvyat vpoket omēpen estaklikin...

Hvtvm arvtet ervlakvntvs. Momet okat, Vyehpvyēs kontskeko? maken... Vyehpvyēt os komit omisat, taklikit omis, kicin... Momat, Estomehcet vpeswv 'svyvranetska? maken... Estomehcit 'svyetv ker-rvkot estaklikit omis, kicin... Vpeswv celayetv tis cekẹrresekot on omeko? maket omisat... Eco-hvrpen avm vpoyvs cē, mahken, iem vpoh-yin... Eco-hvrpe hẹren 'tohpvtapicet hẹret vpohyet momehcet, hvtvm vpeswvo matvpomēcet hẹren vpoyet ocet, hẹren 'tohweteknēn vpoyēpet hẹren vm etetakuehcet... Hokvs, maket, cụtkusē etetakkvyusvkē tạyusēn vnhahyen... Momusen, Eccv-fvkvn avmes, mahken, iehmin, hẹren 'svwvnahyet, cụtkusen vnhahyen... Momusen, Tokvs, mahket, avntaklihcet okat, Yefulketskat, ayet cencuko eroretskat, cuko ofv tokon takhvkēn min erohwvkehcet erecēyetskvrēs. Moman cenhok-tvlwv tat cenhomecē hẹret totkv tempen taklikẹpen eroretskvrēs. Mont okat, Vpeswuce estọmusat vnheckusēt omisekv, eraehset, noricvs, kicetskvrēs. Momen mvn cenhomecēt, takliket omvtētis, mv momē

around... Then the person who had lent me the bow, the one I had seen before, came once more and said to me, You don't even know how to handle a deer, do you? That's true. As I have not been killing deer, I don't know how to handle a deer, to dress it and skin it, I said... He stood awhile, and then he came forward to where the deer lay... Wait! he said, and skinned them for me and threw them to me... Now. Take care of them, he said to me as he departed, and then I started to secure them... Then he said, You may leave anytime you want, and left... Then I took care of my deer meat and stayed awhile, though I ought to have left, since the children are hungry and [my mother-in-law] is angry with me, I thought... So I started to prepare, gathering the deer meat... I didn't know how I could take all the meat, though I had tied it all together, and there was so much, I had gathered and stacked so much, that I just sat there...

Again the man came back. Then he said, You aren't thinking of leaving, are you? I thought I ought to be leaving but I'm just sitting around here, I said... But how are you going to take the meat? he asked... I don't know how I'm going to take it, that's why I'm still here... You really don't know how to handle meat, do you? he asked... Put the deerskins over here for me, he said, and I put them there... He stacked the skins neatly on top of one another, then he stacked the meat the same way, then he packed [the meat] tightly together and got it ready for me... Now, he said, and made small bundles that could be connected together... Then he said, Hand me the bowstring, and I gave it to him, and he tied it securely, making it small for me... Then he said, Now, and as he set it down for me, he said, When you go, you will keep going until you get to your house, and lay your pack at the side rather than inside, and go in. Now your mother-in-law is still very angry at you, and will be sitting by the fire when you get there. And you will say, I have gotten a little meat, so go get it and cook it, he said.

kicetskan vtēkusen, ēsso 'svmokoteticē on atasiket, rahēcan, mvn wvnvkusēt ohlikan rienrecvpvrēs, cvkicen omvnkan...

Momvranen okēpen vnhoktvlwv tat cvpakkē hērē omēt taklikēpen erecēyiyit... Vpeswuce omusat estomusat vnheckusēt omisan omekv, noricvs, kihcen... Momusen 'svmokotecicē ont, atasiket ayat, mvn vpeswv wvnvkē yohwvkēcvyan rienrecapan, afvtosiket, tepiket, cuko hospvn 'svnvfiken, selaksēket arvcokvntvs, makesasvtēs, mahokvnts cē.

And even though she is sitting there angry at you, as soon as you say that, she will jump up fast enough to raise dust, and when she goes to look, she will untie the bundle there, he said to me...

And it happened as he said, my mother-in-law was sitting there very angry when I went in... I have gotten a little meat, so cook it, I said... And then she jumped up fast enough to raise dust, and when she untied the bundled meat that I had placed there, it kicked back, slapped her, and hit her against the wall of the house, and she went around screaming, someone once said, it was said.

25

Hunter taken to the deer cave

A hunter stalks a doe, who asks him why he is stalking her and her fawns. She leads him back to a big cave where there is every imaginable deer. They allow him to stay until mating season approaches. Since he lacks a coat and headpiece, they lend him a deerhide and antlers and send him out with a doe. He is attacked by another deer and stripped of his coat, but they lend him another. Then he is shot and his coat is taken again, so they send him away, he finds his gun, and he becomes human again.

In reversing roles and becoming a deer, the hunter tries to live as deer do, but fails miserably.

Este hvmket Fayvyēt arvyvntvs, makesasvtēs, mahokvnts. Mont omet fayet arvyisan, eco-ecket 'cucvlke 'sēyvpvyepēt nanopet akhvyakpēt ocēt omvntvs, pelofv vfopken... Mvn erorvyan, mvn aknanopēpet eco-ecke ecucvlke 'sēyvpvyusēt 'sak-vrēpen hehcit... Momusen vyopkit ayit omvyan cvhecvkē 'svmmont oman, pefatkekut akfullet omen, vneu vyopkit omikv, vneu ayvyē monket, vwolēn erorin, eco-ecket okat, Iepuyopket ometskeko? Mv epuyopkat wihket, mont eccvo wvkehcet avtes! cvkicet omen... Vyopkvyvtē wihket momusen oh-ayit erorin okat, Pucak-ahyetsken, puncukon vpeyvkēs, cvkicaket omen... Momētis os, kihcin... Mon omat, vpēyvkēs, mahket, vpeyēpen vcak-ayvyvntvs.

Mont fullet omeyisan, ēkvn-hvoke-rakkot ocēt omvten, mvn vwēpēt fullēpet ohkvten eroriceyvntvs. Mont eroriceyan, Naket estomen resestem awatskehaks? kihocen... Estonkut omis. Epuyopket omen resawet ohmēs, makaken... Mont omat, likvtētis. Estomvranan omēs, cvkicakvntvs.

Momat mv ēkvn-hvoke-rakko resecēyeyat mv ofv tat mvn eco estomvkēt komvkat mvn wakkepē tayen eco vculvket os komvkat mvn sopakhvtkēpen hēcvyvntvs, makesasvtēs, mahokvnts.

Mont omen, mvn vpakit likvyvntvs, makvtēs. Mon okakat, Fulletvt puncak-vranet onkv mvt punhoyvnehpen, yefulkepvrēs, cvkicaken likvyvntvs.

Mon ayen mv fulletv makakvtē tat oketv cakket os, makakvntvs. Momat mvt eco hosaklan okahkvt hakvntvs. Mon momusen mv vretv makakvtē tat momusen cakket os makaket fullvntvs. Moman kapvn ocetskekut omēpekv kapv tat cem pvleyvrēs. Momet 'sekohlikvo escem pvleyvrēs,

I was going about hunting, someone once said, it was said. As I was hunting, I came to a clearing and saw a doe with her little fawns grazing in a clearing commonly found along a wooded area... As I approached, I spotted the doe grazing about with her little fawns... And I crept up on them and felt as though they could see me, but they didn't run and kept grazing, and I kept on creeping closer and closer, and as I got near, the doe said, You're creeping up on us, aren't you? Quit creeping up on us, lay that gun down, and come here! she said to me... So I quit stalking them and walked over to them, and they said, Go with us and we'll go to our house... All right, I said... Well, then, let's go, she said, and they started going and I went with them.

And as we were going along, we came to a big cave, and that is where they had come from, and we arrived there. And as we arrived, they were asked, Why have you brought someone? It's all right. He was sneaking up on us so we brought him back with us, they said. Well, let him stay awhile. Whatever happens will happen, they told me.

Now inside the cave we had entered were deer of all kinds lying everywhere, obviously old deer, I thought, because I saw they were very grey, someone once said, it was said.

In that way I came to live with them, he said. Then they said, It is getting to be time for our get-together, so when that is over, he can return home, they said, and I stayed.

Time went by and they said that the time for the get-together that they had spoken of was approaching. What they had been talking about was mating time. Suddenly one day they went about saying the day had arrived to go. Now since you don't have a coat, we'll lend you a coat.

cvkicakvntvs. Mon mvn okvkēpekv, eco-hoktē tat hvmkusvnton em ossi-
hocen... Mont eco-honvnwvo hvmkusētan ossihocvnton, momusen hoktē
tat awihekvntut essumecēpen, vpǫkeyisan... Momusen, Kapv tat yvn
kaket os, mahket, avnkahohyen omat, mvt eco-hvrpen okahkvtet avmhoh-
yen vciyit... Mon Heyvn 'sekohlikvo esliket os, cvkihcet, mvo asvmhoyan,
mvt eco yvpe estvmǫhet omen okhohyvtet, mvo 'svmhohyen mvo estv-
mǫhen 'sekohlicit, vm etetahket ohmen... Momusen hoktē tat avm ossicv-
ranet vm punayet okat, Fayvlket tǫyet ont omis fulletv mvt cakkēpet
omēpekv, fuliyēn hoyanē ylket omētok, mvt momvranet ont os. Momen
heyv kapv cem paleyat vcayēcēt eshueretskvrēs. Momen Cvrahohekon
kont hēre mahēn ēyvketēcē hēret aret ometskvrēs. Momen hvtvm heyv
hoktē cem ossicvraneyat eco-honvntake ētv sasat 'secepenkvlēcetvn
komet orēn escetepohoyvrēs. Momis cēmeu estofvn 'Svcvpenkvlēcekon
kont orēn cēmeu ietepoyet esaret ometskvrēs, cvkicet... Momen tǫyen vm
punayet cvmomehcet... Momusen eco-hoktē tat avm ossihohcen,
momusen vneu vcohsihohcen vtehkehkit 'sayvyat momusen mvn vcak-
arin omvyisan, mvn momepvranen okephoyen, eco-honvnwvt vrēpvtēs
komvken 'svcvfaccet omēpat mv hoktē 'sarvyan 'svcvpenkvlēcetvn
eyahcen... Momusen mvt momet ont on omat estetepoyetskvrēs mahket,
vm punahohyet omēpvnkekv, momusen vneu ietepoyit omit, mvo iesem
vkoslvyē vlket omit... Esvrēpit omvyvnkan, pvhcē mahē ylkusen
hoyvnēcēn, Nake tat estohmē ont os kont omvyat, estomē 'svm momat
ercepētkvyan, 'tetǫn avm vrotakkuehcet ayusin resvcvwikehpet ohmen
wǫkkin... Momusen entakhakv estvmǫhet vrēpet omehpvtet esvcohsv-
yaklet 'svcaret, momusen vm vsatehpet, kapv tat, momusen vncvwehpet
momusen esvkuyiket mv kapv tat ē fekēppican erhuyirit vyēpvyvntvs,
makesasvtēs.

And we'll lend you a headpiece, too, they told me. So just as they had
said, they began to let the does come out one at a time... Then they would
let out just one buck, and then the buck would follow the doe and they
would disappear together as we sat... Then they said, Here is the coat,
tossing it to me, and they had meant a deerskin, so they gave it to me and
I put it on... And they said to me, Here is the headpiece, and handed that
to me also, and it was some wonderful antlers that they had lent me, and
I put all of this finery on and was ready... Then, as they were going to let
the female out, they talked to me, saying, At this time there are many
hunters, but the get-together is approaching, and we always do it until
everything is done, so we will this time, too. Now you must take care of
this coat we are lending you as long as you wear it. And take care that
you don't get shot. And again there are other young bucks out who will
want to take away from you this female we are sending out and who will
fight you for her. But you will not want anyone to take her from you and
you will fight back, they told me... And they spoke much to me... And
then they let the doe out for me, and I was allowed to come out and went
right behind her, and as we went awhile, just as I was told would happen,
a buck came out from somewhere and came to meet me, and he wanted
to take the female I had away from me... And then because they had told
me that I should fight back if that happened, I fought back and seemed to
be getting the better of him every time... As we were passing through tall
grass, I thought, Something is not right, and as soon as I sensed it, coming to an abrupt stop, I felt a hard blow that brought me down and I lay
there... It had been [a buck] with a huge rack of antlers and he stood
straddling me, and he tore my coat, took it from me, moved away with it,
and as he stood there shaking it out, I departed, someone once said.*

* The word *fekēppican* sounds as though it refers to shaking, though its meaning is uncertain.

Momen vyẹpvyat arit mv ēkvn-hvoke-rakko erorin oman, mv kapv vm palē fullvtē tat vpokẹpen erorvyvntvs. Mon okat, Kapv tat cencvwephoyehaks? makaken... Vncvwēpet omhos, kicin... Hvtvm cem pvleyvrē tis os, cvkicakisat, momusen hvtvm kapv tat vm pvlhohyen momusen hvtvm ayvyvntvs makvtēs.

Mont arin mv vretv ocakē makakvtē tat hoyvnvkē poken fullēn sụlkēn retohkvlkaket fullen nanopet akhvyakpē oklanạkusan akfullen... Nake tat estos komēsko omēt on omis omē ont here mahet ēyvketēcvyēt arvyēt omvtētat nanopkvn 'svm vhēret oklanakan vcvnokset 'sak-arin, hvtvm atvpockat hvtvm vm vrahhet resvcvwihket... Hvtvm mv kapv vm pvlhoyvtē tat hvtvm vncvwehpet hvtvm mv kapv vncawat ētan 'sahyet fekēppican, hvtvm erhuyirit vyẹpvyat vrẹpit, hvtvm mv cuko arvyvtē ervlakvyan, hvtvm kapv tat cencvwephohyehaks? cvkicen... Vn cvwēpet omhos, kicin... Mon omat mucv tat tayēpēs omētok yefulkepetskvrēs. Tạyen kapvn punyvmahkuecētt ometskekv, vyepvccvs cvkihocet omvnken... Momusen Vyēpetskēs cvkihohcet omet avcohsihohcen... Momusen ervtēpvyat arit mv eco vyopkvyē esarvyē eccv wvkēcvyvtē mv ēkvnv kẹrrusvyē monkat omētok erorvyan mv eccv tat lekwēpvtēt wakkẹpvten... Eresehpit arit vyẹpvyat vncuko hakusat erorit omvyis, cvhonecepē hakētt vrẹpvyvtēt omēpvtētok, cuko ervlakvyat cvpenkalēt svokē hayvyvntut, taskē hayvyēto estomis mv arvyvtē omēt vrvko tayet omis omikv, taskē hayit arit estọmvko tayet arit fekhonnvyvntvs, makesasvtēs, mahokvnts cē.

And as I was going I came to the big cave and arrived where the ones who had lent me the coat were sitting. And they asked, Was your coat taken from you? It was taken from me, I said... We'll lend you another, they told me, and they lent me another coat and again I continued on, he said.

And I was still there and the get-together that they spoke of was over and a great many came together and were grazing in the fresh green clearing... Though it appeared everything was all right, I always watched myself, but I became greedy grazing on the fresh green grass, and then a shot caught me on the side and knocked me down... Again the coat that they lent me was taken from me and again the one that took my coat moved away and shook it, and again I got up and left, and again I came to the place where I had been living, and again they asked, Was your coat taken from you? It was taken from me, I said... Well, this time is enough: you may now return home. Because you have wasted so many of our coats you must go, they said to me... Then they told me, You may leave, and they put me out... Then as I was on my way back, I remembered the country where I had stalked the deer and had laid my gun down, and when I got there, the gun was still there and very rusty... I got it and as I neared my house, I knew that I had become wild going about, and coming home, I was scared and snorting, and I tried to jump but could not as I used to, I could not go about as before, I tried to jump and could not, and so settled down, someone once said, it was said.

26

Man races a lizard

Two men go hunting and one discovers a lizard with eggs. The other man wishes to race her. The lizard chases him, but eventually becomes so exhausted that she climbs into her nest and dies.

Many Creek stories involve competitions between animals (stories 3, 9) or between a man and an animal (stories 12, 26).

Fayet este hokkolet welakvtēs. Momen fayē welakat, mv hvmket este okhacē hēṛēt omvtēs. Moman mv hvmket fayē arvtē ervlakat, Vcoklepv kayat eslikvcoks, kicet yem onayen... Estvmvn omen omat ervm onvyvs: Enletkvranis, kicet oman... Kos, nake holwvyēcēt omēs, monkv est' ēsēt omēs. Monkv herekot omētan oketskes, kicet, erem onvyetv eyacekot oman, mv este hvmkat, estohmen vwicēceko tayēpet omen... Mont on omat, er cem onayvyētis okis, kihcet, vcak-ayvtēs.

Mon welaken mv nake eshuerē hēcvtē erorhoyvtēs. Momen Vsin okv-yvnken: aossēt avwakket os, kicen... Ossēt estvmạhet avwakken erem onayvtēs. Mon mvn enletketvn eyacēpet okēpekv, momusen em etetakeh-pet accvkē tat omẹlkvn ēkayehpet, momusen oh-ayet ayet ervwolicat, nak kicen omētok, hvlvlạtket ahvtvpiket assehcet ohmen... Es ayat pohkusat pihket cvyayahken... Estvn esēpis omēs, komit huervyof, hvtvm estọmusēt pohken, hvtvm rapihkacoken pohit, huerin pohkv hēṛen yepihkē hahken, huerin aret ohkvtet hoyanet oman... Mv vcoklepvo cakkusen yesvhohyet oman, mv este tat mv vcoklepv-hute hueran rem vfulotket ostihcet oman, mv vcoklepv tat cakkusen mv eto vfulotkat, osticat cakkusen mv eto vfulotkat ostihcet, hvtvm enletiken essumhokehpen... Huerin ayen hvtvm mont omisekv hvtvm estomuset pihken hvtvm pihkvcoken, pohit huerin, ayet yvwolicat pohkv hēṛen pihkē haken... Huerin ayen, esvrēpen okeh-pvtet, mvn mont omisekv, mv cakkusē 'sarat emonkuset eresvlaket yeshoyahnen huerin, Mv este tat mvn momēcet omisekv... Hvtvm mv vcoklepv-hute ervfulotket ostihcet, hvtvm hoyahnet enletiken... Hvtvm 'svhoyehpen mvn em ehakit huerin... Mont omisekv hvtvm estomusēt pohken, hvtvm rapihkacoken pohit huerin... Momet omēpisekv eswelv-kẹpet okehpvtet 'svtuccēnat tat mv este mit estomusat 'mvhopvyēcepusē hakepēn yesvhohyet ohmen... Mv vcoklepv-hute eto huerat tat vfulotket ostihcet, mv este tat rahēcet huerisat, mv vcoklepv eroren, hvtvm enletiken 'svhoyet omis, mv vcoklepv tat hotusēpet omētok, hvwaklusē

Two men were out hunting. And of the two who were hunting, one was a very funny person. When one of the hunters returned from a hunting trip, he said, There's a lizard that's laying eggs... Wherever she is, go show me: I want to run from her, [the other] insisted. No, she's very mean and catches people. So you're talking about something bad, he said, and he didn't want to tell him, but the one hunter couldn't get [the other] to give up the idea... Well, all right, I'll go show you, he said, and went with him.

So they went and arrived at the place where he had seen the thing standing. That's where I meant: she had come out and was lying there, he said... She had come out and was lying there, awesomely huge, and he went over and told her. Now he really wanted to run from her, so he began to get ready, taking off all his clothes, and went toward her, drawing near, and whatever it was he said to her, she slowly came down and began to chase him... As he led her in pursuit, you could hear him whooping, and then it grew quiet... He might have been caught, I thought as I stood there, and again I could hear him faintly, then I could hear him whooping in the distance as I stood there, the whooping became clearly audible as I stood there and as he passed... The lizard had almost caught up with him as they went by, the man went around for the fourth time where the lizard's tree stood, and the lizard was catching up as [the man] went around the tree, the fourth time he went around the tree she had almost caught him, and he ran from her again as they went out of sight... I kept standing and time went by, again as before I heard him whooping faintly, whooping as I stood there, and as they came closer, he became clearly audible as he whooped... And then after a while, as it was before, [the lizard] was almost up with him still, and as they came back by again, I stood there, as the man had been doing... Again he went around four times where the lizard's nest stood, and again he passed by, running from her... Again they passed by, I stood there waiting... As before, there was a faint sound, then I heard haket yehoyahnen oman... Hvtvm essumhoket omen huervyisan hvtvm pihkacokisat... Mv este tat homv-mahen vrēpet ohmvtet, mv este vcok-lepv-hute hvtvm vfulotket ostihcet hoyanet omis, mv vcoklepv-rakko tat svsekot omisat... Vrēpat ohmvtet hotusepvtēt hvwakluset estvmahet lekvkappet hoyahnet ayet mv ehute hueran erorat mv ehute hoyvnekot, ayusonkot vliket mv ehute vcemiken... Mv enlētkē arat ra atet ervlahken rvthoyeyvntvs. Mon okat, Estohma, mv vcoklepv-kayv? maken... Vsin ehuten ervcemiks, kicin... Mon omat, elēpēs, makvntvs. Mon okat, Cesvrēs, cvkicetskvnkat, 'mvkoslusvyan oketskvten, cvseko tayuset ehute yvcemkēpet omvcoks. Monkv elēpēs, maken, ervthoyeyvntus maket onayesasvtēs, mahokvnts.

Momat mv eto vcoklepv-hute vcemkvtē eto tat tenēpusē hayepēt ont... Nake estomis vyocet yesvcemkvt omētok: nak esse tis, tafv oman okis... Nake em mokkē tylkusēn mv eto huericet omvntvs, makesasvtēs, maket okhoyvnts cē.

whooping, as I stood... Then the same thing happened, as they came for the third time, and this time the person was a little bit ahead as they went by... Then when he went around the tree where the lizard's nest was for the fourth time, and stood looking back, the lizard came along, and he took off running again and they went, but the lizard was tired and had her mouth hanging open as she went by... Once again they went out of sight and as I stood there I heard whooping again... The man had gotten way ahead, and he went around the lizard's nest again four times and passed by, but the big lizard was not there... Finally she came by all tired out, mouth open, body all shiny, and went to the tree where her nest was, but didn't go on, and barely going, she climbed up to the nest... And the one that ran from her came back and we both came back. Where is the lizard that was giving birth? he asked... She climbed up to her nest over there, I said... Then she died, he said. You told me that she would get me, but I got the best of her and she could not get me and has climbed into her nest. So she died, he said, and we came back, someone once told, it was said.

And [the lizard] had made the tree where she had climbed into her nest very smooth... She had gathered all kinds of things and brought them back to the nest: fur, feathers, and such... The tree stood covered with pollen and dust, someone once said, it's been said.

27
Turtle tries to look up women's dresses

Turtle wants to look up women's dresses and digs a hole under a door. He is seen and beaten. The turtle sings a song so that his shell comes back together. Then he hides under the pounding bowl and makes lewd remarks as the women pound corn. The women find him but are unsure this time how to kill him. Following his suggestion, they make a necklace of their body hair and throw him into the water. He reappears on the other side and they taunt each other. Raccoon then asks Turtle how he acquired his human ways. Turtle says it's from beating his grandmother. Raccoon kills his own grandmother and is left mute. When he blows his nose, a crow appears and flies off.

This story explains why turtle shells appear broken (as in story 7), why raccoons are mute, and why crows are noisy. Turtle here sings a slightly different version of the song in story 7. Margaret Mauldin sees the last part as saying "Be careful who you believe, you might act on false information."

Lucvt hoktvken honnv-ofvn enhecetvn eyacet arvtēs. Mont aret omet estohmet omatet hecē tayen omat mvn oh-vkerricet vrēpvtet... Vhvoke lecvn ēkvnvn korrēpet, mvn vsumkēt liket ometvn eyacet omet... Momusen mvn vkerrickv em etetaket onkv, momusen mvn yelikvtēs. ēkvnv yewosehpet mvn ēyakpikvtēs.

Mont mvn liket omis hechoyekon likēpet vcewepē haken eshechoyvtēs. Mohmet eraehset, nafket cetakkusēn hahoyvtēs. Mont ervwihokvtēs. Moman tvkoca-catucet enlasēpet omen, momusen mv lucv tat yvhiket okat:

> Cvte-li-li,
> Cvte-li-li,
> Cvte-sokoso,
> Cvte-li-li,
> Cvte-sokoso,

maket liket, mv nafkē cetahkē ervwihokat omvlkvt etelikē pokēpet... Eravtēpet hvtvm keco elecvn mvn hvtvm matvpomēn yewosēpet, mvn akpikēpet omet... Hvtvm mvn hoktvket vcen hocat, Heh! makē omēt vce tat hocēpet omhoyvntok, mv mahokof, mv lucvt okat matvpomēn maket, Heh! Cena-esse! maket omen... Estvn naket okehaks? komet hopoyet omhoyis, estvn okat kerrekot omet, wikvntot, hvtvm vce hocēpat, hvtvm, Heh! mahokof, matvpomēn maket okat Heh! Cena-esse! makēpet omen... Hopoyet omhoyvtētan, mv keco huerat mahe omen okēpet omen, mv kecon vkuehoyan, mv keco huerat mahusan, ēkvnvn sofecepēt taklikēpet okehpvten eshehcet momusen elēcetv komet omakat estomēcaket elēcvkē tayen omat maket lihocvtēs.

There once was a turtle who wanted to look up women's dresses. He went about wondering for quite a while what he could do to see what he wanted to see. [He decided] he'd dig a hole under the door, and would sit buried in the hole... Then, with his plan ready, he immediately came and sat there. He dug a hole and got in it.

And he sat there unseen for a time, and then after a long while someone found him. Then they pulled him out and beat him to a pulp. And they threw him away. Then a little red ant licked his wounds, and the turtle began to sing:

> I come-come together,
> I come-come together,
> I shake-shake together,
> I come-come together,
> I shake-shake together,

he sang as he sat, and all the crushed and broken pieces they had thrown away came back together... He came back and this time dug in the same way under the pounding bowl, and got in... And when the women pounded the corn, it was customary for all the women to say Heh! as the corn was pounded, so when they said that, the turtle would repeat after them, Heh! Your body hair!... Who is saying that? they wondered and looked around, but couldn't find where it was coming from and would quit [looking], and when the pounding started and they said Heh! again, he would repeat by saying, Heh! Your body hair! They searched, and as it had come from around where the pounding bowl stood, they moved it, and right where the pounding bowl stood, they found he had dug a deep place and had been down there saying those things, and then right away they wanted to know how they could kill him, so they held him captive.

Moman mv lucv arē nafkē cetahkē rvwihokvtē ētat omēpet omen mvn kerraket... Momēn mvn nafket cetakkusēn hahyet ervwikakvtē ētan, hvtvm matat rvlvkēpet likēpet omehpvten kerraket omet, estomēcēt omvkat elēcvkē tayat? kicet okakat... 'Lehayvn uewvn vcahnet, morehcet, mvn akpikvkēs, kihocen, okat, Momusat akhosēlit kvsvppuecvyēt omēs. Naket mvtat 'svm estonkot omēs, makēpen, Mvo eston momēcēpis okēpēs, kont omet, estomēcetv kerrekot licet omet... Hvtvm okat, Totkvn taklicvkēs! kicaken... Mvo, takhosēlit vslēcvyēt omēs, mvo, kicen, Mvo estvn momēcepē tayusēt os, kicaket, estomēcetv kerrekot licaken... Okat, Ena-essen lehmet, cvnocihcet, uewvn resvcakwihokan, calusats, maket omen, hoktvket alehmet, enocihcet, uewvn eresakwikakvtēs.

Momen uewv ofvn 'sakcēyiyet oksētecicet 'svyēpet 'sak-vhopvyēcehpet eresak-osiyet tvpalvn resossen hecaket ehvnaket okat... Mvn momēn cvmēhocen omat, calusats! mahken... Mvtis nokkētut omis alehmēt enocihcēs estomis kont... Mvn kvyaklē ont resosset okēs ta! kicaken... Mv 'secohcemkvyē escvkvyaklate mvn cvkvyaklētut omētvnks! mahket, Walose, walose kahi! mahket, 'svyēpvtēs.

Mont mvn nake enucepēt 'sarof, wotkot 'svfaccvtēs. Mont em pohen, Este 'mvretvn estenheckēpēt os, kicen... Estomēt ohmen cenhēckehaks? kicen... Este-puse hoktaluse ocēpvkat, mvn taknafket omvkis, kihcen... Ayat epuse hoktaluse licēt omat, Wotko tat momusen ahyet, mv epuse hoktalusat ernafkvtēs. Mont elēcēt omat, hvtvm mvn onvyetvn kont aret,

Now they knew that this was the same turtle that was beaten, crushed to a pulp and thrown away... He was beaten to a pulp, and thrown away, and the same one had returned and was sitting there, they knew now, so they asked, How can we kill him? Put water in a kettle, boil it, and put him in it, they said, and he said, That's nothing. I can urinate in it and cool it off. Things like that don't bother me, he said, so they thought, He just might be able to do what he said, and didn't know what to do with him as they kept him... Again they said, Let's put him in the fire! I can also urinate on the fire and put it out, he said, so they said, He just might be able to do it, and didn't know what to do with him as they kept him... Then he said, Pluck out your body hair, put it around my neck, throw me in the water, and I'll die, and the women plucked out their body hair, put it around his neck, and threw him in the water.

Then he went into the water creating a wake across the top, went a long way out, and seeing him come out on the opposite bank, they scolded him...* When they do that to me, I just die! he said... It really does hurt, though, to pluck [hair] out, and we did it and hung it around his neck, thinking it had to be... Look at that bowlegged thing, they said, coming out over there saying that! I bow my legs when I climb up on you! he said, and said Wa-lo-si Wa-lo-si ka-hay! as he left with the hair.

As the turtle was going around with the thing around his neck, a raccoon met him. He asked him [about the things around his neck], and [Turtle] said, With these you develop human ways... How did you get them? he asked... I have an elderly grandmother and I beat her, he said... And immediately Raccoon went to where his elderly grandmother lived and

---

* The word *oksētecicet* seems to refer here to making a wake. A related word *oksētkē* is used in a similar way at the end of story 10. These words remind Margaret Mauldin of the word *sētetv* 'to rip'.

cuko likēn eroret omat, Waluset! maket ēti naken makeko tayet eshueren... Naken onvyetvn ocvken omat, rēsikvkēs okattan os, kihocen, rēskan, osahwvt omvten, Kak! Kak! mahket tvmkvtēs.

beat her.* And having killed her, and wanting to tell, he went and arrived at a house, and said, Wa-lo-sit! and could not say anything else as he stood there... If you've got something to say, blow your nose, they said, and when he blew, it was a crow, and it said, Kak! Kak! and flew away.

* The expression *epuse hoktạluse* means 'elderly grandmother' to Margaret Mauldin and Juanita McGirt. It might also have been a way to say 'great-grandmother'.

28

Wolf wants to become spotted

Wolf wants to be spotted like Fawn. Fawn has him get under a basket and lie in the fire, then burns him up and gathers his bones. Another wolf chases him, but he hides under one woman's dress, in another's earthen pot, and in a third's nose. Wolf discovers Fawn each time and hires Turtle to shoot him. Wolf wishes to pay Turtle with some of the meat, but Turtle rejects every part except a small blood clot. He tells his wife to prepare it, but she slaps it in his eyes and makes his eyes red. (cf. Swanton 1929, Creek story 34).

There are two main parts to this story. In the first part, Fawn is saved by his ingenuity, but Wolf's clan finds revenge. The second part about Turtle is often told separately, and suggests that the turtle's red eyes (and his love of water) resulted from his pickiness. Stories 27 and 28 both involve powerful charms made from the hair or bones of one's enemies.

Yvhvt eco-tokohucen 'tefaccvtēs. Momen Yvhvt em pohet okat, Nake 'stohmen momēt cetokohē cehakvthaks? Yvhvt maket eco-tokohucen em pohvtēs. Mon eco-tokohucet okat, Turrakkon vm vpotuehcet, ohmet est em oh-etechoyen, ayen mv est em oh-etechoyat omylkvt est ohnekrē pohiken on omat, mvt tokohat estehaket ont omētvnks, ecucet kicvtēs.

Mon mvn Yvhvt tokohē haketvn eyacet aret okekv, momusen, Estomēcēt omhoyēton oketskat, cvmomēcetsken, mv cena tokohē 'saretskat omusēn cvhakvrēn cvyacēs, kicen... Mon omat, pakse tat mvn cem etetakuecarēs, kihcet... Mont estvmvn omvranan mvo em onahyet omaten... Yvhv tat momusen tokohusē haketvn eyacet omēpekv, hvyatkat momusen vyēpvtēs. Mv ēkvnv em melhoyat erorepvtēt wakkēpen, 'cuce tat yopvn rorvtēs.

Mont mv estokohvranat, turrakko ocepēt erohret... Momusen, Heyvn takwakketsken, turrakon ecepotuehcit omvranvyēt ont os, kicen... Mv yvhv tat tokohē haketvn orēn eyacetut omekv, momusen, Yvn takwakkvs, kihocat, vkvsamuset estentakwakkvtēs.

Mon mvn okekv, mv turrakko vpotuehcet, eto rahopoyēpet, yemoh-vpoyet sulkēn hahyet, momusen em vhetēcvtēs.

Momen mv yvhv tat tokohē haketvn eyacet omekv, mv totkv ofv wakken, nēkrē vyēpat, mv yvhvo resvhētken... Cvnokres! Estomvhanihaks? maket, yvhv tat mv totkv ētkat ofv mahen takpiket oken... Mvt momēto estomis vliketskvrēs. Mvt cetokohicat omētis os, kicet, mv eco-tokohuce tat huerēpen... Hvtvm, Cvholvnē tayēpan os. Mvtv estomvranihaks? maken... Mvo mvt cemont on omat, matan takholvnvs, kicet mv eco-tokohuce tat huerēpvtēs.

Wolf met a spotted fawn. And Wolf asked the little deer, What did you do to make yourself spotted? And the spotted fawn answered, They put a corn riddle over me, then they build a fire on it, and when everything is burned and the fire goes out, that's when you come out spotted, the fawn said.

And Wolf wanted to be spotted, so he said, Whatever you say they did to you, you do the same to me, I want to become spotted like you... Well, then, I'll get it ready for you tomorrow, [the fawn] said... And he also told him where it would be... Now Wolf wanted to be spotted so badly that as soon as morning came, he left. He got to the designated place and lay down, and the fawn got there after him.

And to make the spots, he had come with a corn riddle... Then [the fawn] said, Lie down here and I'll place the corn riddle over you... The wolf wanted so badly to become spotted that when he was told to lie down, he immediately lay down trustingly.

Then as he said, [the fawn] put the corn riddle over him, fetched wood, and piled it on top, piling it very high, and then started the fire.

And the wolf still wanted so badly to be spotted, that he lay in the fire, and as the fire spread, the wolf began burning, too... I'm burning! What do I do now? Wolf asked as he lay right where the fire was burning... Even though it's like that you'll stay with it. That's what makes you spotted, the spotted fawn said as he stood by... Then again [Wolf said], I'm about to defecate. Now what am I going to do? he said... If it happens to you, just go ahead and defecate there, said the little spotted deer as he continued to stand.

Momen vyēpen, hvtvm cvhoselvrąnos os. Mvtv estomvranihaks? kicen...
Matan takhoselvs. Mont omvkvnts, kicen... Matan takhosēlet takwakket,
hvtvm, Cvlepē tayē omēhakēs, kicen... Mvo mvt cetokohē ayat
respokepvranet omētis os, kicvtēs. Mon takwakket nokrēt okvtētok
matan takwakket tak-elēpvtēs.

Momen ayen, mv totkv vslēpoken ratakhēcan, yvhv-fune tat tak-ocen
eshecehpet, momusen mv ecucet tak-vteloyvtēs. Mont wvnvyēpet
enucēt 'sarvtēs. Mont okat esyvhiket 'sarvtēs. Mon yvhiket okat hvm-
makvtēs:

> Yvhv-fune kvrkap,
> Yvhv-fune kvrkap,
> Sule tis mermer,

maket yvhiket 'svrēpof, yvhvt esvfaccvtēs. Mon okat, Naken makēn
yvhiket oketskehaks? kicen... Cvpuset maket yvhiken pohvyvntat, mvn
vkerricvyat cvpǫhyakusē ont omet, yvhikit arit okis, kicen... Mon omat,
yvhiketsken pohvranis, kicen... Mvn maket okis. Okekv, enyvhikvtēs.
Mont okat,

> Yvhv-fune kvrkap,
> Yvhv-fune kvrkap,
> Sule tis mermer,

And as time went on, again he said, I am about to urinate. What am I
going to do? he asked... Just urinate where you are. That's what one does,
he said... So he urinated as he lay there, and again he said, I feel like I am
going to die... You're almost through getting spotted, [the fawn] said.
[Wolf] lay there and burned and continued to lie there and died.

And awhile later, the fire died down and [the fawn] went to look, and
what he saw was the wolf's bones there, and then the fawn gathered them
up. And he tied them and wore them about on his neck. And he sang
about it as he went around. And when he sang, he said this:*

> Wolf bones are dry,
> Wolf bones are dry,
> Even buzzards flap,

and when he was going around singing this, a wolf met him. And [this
new wolf] said, What are you saying when you sing? I used to hear my
grandmother sing this, and when I think about her, I get very lonesome,
[the fawn] said, so I'm singing it... Well, then, I want to hear you sing,
[the wolf] said... And as he had been singing, he sang for him. [Wolf]
meant it, so [the fawn] sang for him. And he said,

> Wolf bones are dry,
> Wolf bones are dry,
> Even buzzards flap,

---

* Another version of this song is discussed in Kroeber (1981) and is usefully compared to versions
recorded by Tuggle (in Swanton 1929:39) and Wagner (1931:39). Here the song seems to be a hex,
describing (and bringing about) the decay of Wolf's body: bones, buzzards, and in the Tuggle version,
flies and worms. In the Wagner version, it is a boast: "The wolf is bones only . . . but I am spotted."

maket yvhiket okatet ohkvtet yvhiket omen... Mv yvhv-vcule tat vketēcet aret okekv, Heyv hvmmakē yvhiketskat pulēcetvt aret ometskes. Mv nake enocetskat, naken ontskehaks? kicen... Cvpuse tatē 'senockv vnhayvtē celayvkut ocvyēt omētvnket, mvn hvte 'sarit omis, kicen... Mvt mon oketskē onkot os. Monkv pulēcē hēret aret ontskes. Monkv, monkv etohwakkvn kont omis kihcet assehcen, 'svhoyat svhoyen cuko likan mv eco-tokohuce tat enhomvn mv cuko erohret... Momusen, Honnv ofvn cencēyepvranis, hoktēt nak vhorēpet takliket erkicen, okat, Naket estomen aret ontska? kicen... Cvlēcetvn kont vcassēhocen arit omis, kicen... Mon omat, avncēyepvs, kihcen, iencēyēpvtēs. Mont mv hvte encēyekof okat, Vcoh-onahyetskvs, kicvtēs. Momen Mohkotis os, kicvtēs.

Mon hofone-mahekon, hvtvm yvhvt vrēpen okhohyvten vlaket omat, Mvn hopoyit aret omis. Vlvkekathaks? kicen... Hēcvkē sekot os, kicvtēs. Momis mv yvhv-vcule tat mvn vhonwēt 'saret 'svlaket oman okhoyen vlakē tvlkuset omēs. Mont, Estvn estomat kērrētat, vm onvyekot oks, komet, mv yvhv-vcule tat vyeko tayvtēs.

Moman mv ecuce mv honnv ofv ecēyat, nake tis liken omat kērkēt ocēs. Momētut omen, mv yvhv-vcule tat vyeko tayvtēs. Mont omusymmvliken mv hoktē nak vhorē taklikan oket, Ahoyirvs. Naket estomētut on omat mv cenhonnv nake kvwvpē omē ocat, naket on omat hecvranis, kicen... Ahueran, mvn takliket ohmvtēton: mv hoktē ahueran, mvt mv hoktē enhonnv ofvn wakket ohmvtet... Atasiket, enletiken, hvtvm asiyet 'sayet 'svyēpet omen...

Hvtvm matvpomēn cuko likēn hvtvm mv ecuce tat erorvtēs. Mont mvo hoktvlēt mvo nak vhorē tat takliken erem ecēyvtēs. Mont okat, Estvn estomusis iecesokkepvyē tayēs. Momen cvlēcvranet vcassēhocen arit

he sang as he had sung before... The old wolf was very observant and said, This song you're singing is about killing us. That thing around your neck, what is that? he asked... My grandmother made me a necklace and as I have never worn it before, I'm just now wearing it, he said... That's not the way it appears. You're going to kill us. So I want to put a stop to it, he said and chased him, and as they went, the spotted fawn came to a house first... I'm going to get under your dress, he said right away to a woman who was sitting there sewing, and she said, What's the matter? I'm here because they want to kill me and they're chasing me, he said... Well, then, you may get under my dress, she said, and he went under. Before he went in, he said, Don't tell on me. I won't, she said.

Before long the wolf that [the fawn] had talked about arrived. I'm here looking for him. Has he not come by here? he asked... I haven't seen him, she said. But the old wolf had followed the scent and he knew that [the fawn] must have come there. She knows where he is and won't tell me, he thought, and the old wolf would not go.

Now where the fawn had gone under the dress, one could tell something was there. That's how it was, so the old wolf would not go. This continued until he said to the woman who sat sewing, Stand up. I want to see what's making your dress lift up like something's underneath it. I want to see what it is, he said... When she stood up, there [the fawn] sat: when the woman stood up, it had been [the fawn] that had been lying under the woman's dress... He jumped up and started running, [the wolf] gave chase, and they took off...

Again, as before, the fawn came to a house first. And there, too, an old lady sat sewing as he went in. And he said, Can I squeeze in with you somehow? I'm here because they're going to kill me and they're chasing omis, kicen... Mon omat, vsin vrkvswvn akcēyvs! kihcen, mvn erakcēyvtēs. Mont mvn akpikvtēs. Mon mvo kicvtēs, Vcoh-onahyetskvs! kihcet, momusen mv vrkvswv akcēyvtēs. Mont mvn akpiket omis, mvo hesakof, mormokē omēt ocvtēs.

Mon mv yvhv-vcule vrẽpen okhohyvten erohret, momusen erem pohvtēs. Momēn hopoyit arit omis. Vlvkekohaks? kicen... Hẽcvkesekot os, kicvtēs. Momen omēto estomis mvn honwēt 'svlaket omis okhoyekv, vyeko tayet taklikẽpet omisat... Naket estomen heyv osafke eshuerat nak maket okehaks? kicen... Osafket tạyen kvmoksēt ont omis, vpvlv-tvkon estakhueret ont os, kicen... Hiyomen hēcin pvlatetsken hecvranis, kicen... Momusen rastak-ehset, 'susiyet ervpvlatan, mvn akpikēt oman okhohyvten... Erlvtiket hvtvm enletiken, hvtvm assehcet esayat 'sayet oman, hvtvm cuko likēn mv ecuce tat eroret omat... Mvn vcassēcet omhoyen estometv kerrvkot arit omis. Estvn estomusis vcvrvnayvs, kicvtēs. Mont estvn naken vrvnakvkē tayat ọcvyesepekot os, kicet omisat... Mv ecucet okat, Ceyupon cencēyepvranis, kicen... Mon omat, momekvs, kihcen, eyupo-hvoken encēyen mv hoktalat esliken... Hvtvm mv yvhv-vcule eroret okat: Momēn mvn assēcit ohmvyan, yvn vlake ont on vlakit omis, kicet omen... Momis mv hoktē eyupo encēyeko monkof okat, Vcoh-onahyetskvs, kihcet encēyet omēpekv, oh-onvyetv eyacekatēs.

Mont oman mv hoktalat eyupon enhēcvtēs, mv yvhv-vcule yopvn eroret onkv. Mont okat, Mv ceyupo naket cem eston omehaks? kicvtēs. Mon em vyuposket okat, Tạyen cvyupot vnnokiket, vnhvsafket omen taklikit omvyē, kicvtēs. Mon okatet, Mon omat, rēsketsken hecvranis, kihcen...

me, he said... Well, then, get in that earthen pot over there! she said, and he got in. And he sat in it. And again he said, Don't tell on me! and got into the earthen pot. And he sat in there, but when he breathed in and out, there was a bubbling sound.

And the old wolf that he had spoken of got there, and right away questioned her. I'm here looking for him. Did he not come here? he asked... I haven't seen him, she said. Then even so, because he had followed the scent, he would not leave and stayed awhile... Why is this sofkey standing here saying things? he asked...* The sofkey is very sour, but I haven't thrown it out yet, and it's still standing there, she said... While I'm watching, I want to see you throw it out, he said... Then she got the pot of sofkey and took it out, and as she threw it out, [the fawn] was in it and was thrown out... Upon landing, he started running again, and again [the wolf] chased him and they took off, and once again the fawn came to a house first... I'm here because they're chasing me and I don't know what to do. Somehow hide me somewhere, he said. But I have nothing that one can hide behind, she said... Then the fawn said, I'll go in your nose... Well, then, let it be so, she said, and he went into the old lady's nostril as she was sitting... Again the old wolf arrived: I was chasing him and it appears he came here, that's why I've come, he said... But before [the fawn] had gone into the woman's nostril, he'd said, Don't tell on me, and so she didn't want to tell.

Then he looked at the old woman's nose, because the old wolf had arrived afterwards. And he asked, What has happened to your nose? And she answered him, saying, I'm sitting in here because my nose really hurts and is now very swollen. And he said, Well, then, let me see you

* *Osafke* 'sofkey' is a staple food in Creek homes, made by boiling flint corn in a lye solution. It is sometimes allowed to sour.

Rēskan mvn vpiket ohmvten, rēskan vpaket ertaklvtiket hvtvm enletiken, esayat 'sayet oman, hvcce wakkēn vpicēcet vyēpet omen esayvtēs.

Mont oman hvcce onvpusan etot cunēket omat, uewvn aakcunēket ont oman... Mv uewvn akliket os, kont, mv eton vcemket ohliket oman, em vpēttēn hēcet omat, Mvn uewvn akliket os! kont mv uewv tat aktasket... Hotusepvtēt ak-arvtet, eto min ohliket ohmvtet eshēcvtēs.

Mohmet eshehcet omis, estohmet elēceko tayvtēs. Mont omet vhecicvo pvlēpet ont omet, elēhocvrēn eyacet omet, estit elēcē tayat kerrekot omis... Ayen Lucvt likēpen erem orvtēs. Eccv-kotaksen kasēpet likēpen erem orvtēs. Mont okat, Momēn nake elēcetvn vm elēcetskvrēn cvyacet arit omis, kicen... Hvte eccv-kotaksen kasēpusin os, kicen, eratvtēs.

Mont hvtvm yefulket erem orvtēs. Mont hvtvm ervtotvtēs. Momat, Hvte eccv-kotaksen fottayēpusin os, kicen, eratvtēs.

Mont hvtvm komat yefulkvtēs. Mont rem oren, hvtvm ervtoten... Hvte rēn 'mvlvpotēpusin os, kicen eratvtēs.

Mont hvtvm yefulkvtēs. Mont hvtvm erem oret oman, Hvte rēn enkasēpusin os, kicen, eratvtēs.

Mont hvtvm yefulket erem oren okat, Hvte rēn esfottēpusin os, kicvtēs. Mont vcak-vtekon eratvtēs.

blow your nose... When she blew, that's where [the fawn] had been, and as soon as she blew, he fell on the floor, and ran again and they took off, staying close to the edge of the river as they went.

Now over the river was a bowed tree, and it was bent down into the water... He's in the water, [Wolf] thought, and climbed the tree and sat there, but seeing [the fawn's] reflection, he thought, He's in the water! and jumped into the water... He was tired as he went looking around in the water, and then he realized [the fawn] had been sitting in the tree.

And though he found him, there was nothing he could do to kill him. So he hired a guard to watch [the fawn], and he needed someone to kill him, but didn't know anyone who could do it... After a while he came upon Turtle. He came upon him while he was sitting scraping wood for a bow. And he said, There's something I'd like you to kill for me... I'm just now scraping my bow, [Turtle] said, so [Wolf] returned home.

Then again [Wolf] went back [to Turtle]. And again he made his request. I'm just now stringing my bow, [Turtle] said, so [Wolf] returned home.

Then again he decided to go back. And as he got there, he made the request again... I'm just now straightening the arrows, [Turtle] said, and [Wolf] returned home.

Then again he went back. I'm just now scraping the arrows, [Turtle] said, and [Wolf] returned home.

Then again he went back, and when he arrived there, [Turtle] said, I'm just now putting feathers on the arrows. So [Turtle] did not come with him and [Wolf] returned home.

Momet hvtvm yefulket erem oren okat, Hvte rēn 'sem vkotēpusin os, kicen, eratvtēs.

Mont hvtvm yefulkvtēs. Mont yefulket, hvtvm erem oren okat, Acv-cokohyet 'svcvpēhoyen omēpvyētvnks, kicvtēs. Momusen mvn em elēhocvrēn eyacet omekv, momusen acokohyet resatvtēs. Mont esaret resvlahket ohmen, momusen ēccvtēs. Mont ēccat mv rē 'sarvtē omylkvn 'svpvlvtē poyvtēs. Mont okat vsin rē hvmket 'svnsumkvnks. Mvn rasvnhopoyvs, kihcen, ayat mvo eshecē hēret eshehcet, resvlakvtēs. Mohmen mvn rē 'mvhericet aklikvtet, mvn esēccat, mvn esrahvtēs. Mont elehcet ohmen... Mvn okekv, mv elēcē arat enfēkv komet, Ehvfe tis ceyacen omat? kicen... Cvhvfe nokinokusen calusats, maken...* Efulowv tis ceyacen omat? kican, Mvo cvfulowv nokinokusen cvlēpusats, maken... Elupe tis? kicof, Cvlupe nokinokusen calusats, makēpen... Ekv tis? kihocat, Cvkv nokinokusen calusats, makēpen... Enhomehcet, Naken yacekis okeyan omēt'n os! kihcet, naken emekut omylkvn 'tewahlehpet 'svwahephohyen... Momusen cate-tulokfuce cutkusēn ehset, 'to-essen 'svyokkofet mehcet, resatet resvlakvtēs. Mont em puetakeu sulkēt omen resem vlakvtēs. Mon resem oren, Cvrkē! Cvrkē! maket ohpefatken... 'Saret ereslihcet liket omet... Vpeswv tat hecikus oman onkv, ennoricvkēs cē, maket liket omen... Rahechoyan estvmahet 'sohlikēpet omen okēpen... Momusen enrecvphoyan sepekon ayet omen... Estvmvn ocēt omehaks? kihocan... Ofusat, maket liket omētan... Mv eto-esse omylkvn em vwahēhocan, cate-tulokfuce cutkosēt liken hehcet... Heyvt mvtut omehaks? kihocen... Mvn okvyis, maken... Kut, mv momusat cvppucetake 'setetayvrēs, kontskvthakes? kihcet, turwvn mv catē 'sem aktephokvtēt omen momēhohcof, Cvppucetake uewvn 'svm vwaks, maket 'saret... Mvn Lucv turwv cataket omvtēs, mahokvnts.

* The meaning of *nokinokusen* is uncertain.

Then he went back again, and when he arrived there, [Turtle] said, I'm just now trimming the arrows, and [Wolf] returned home.

Then [Wolf] went back. And when he went back, and when he got there, [Turtle] said, Carry me on your back, that's my usual way, he said. Since [Wolf] wanted so badly to have [the fawn] killed, he returned [to where the fawn was] with [Turtle] on his back. When he got back with him, right away [Turtle] shot at [the fawn]. And he shot at him until he used up all the arrows he had brought with him. And he said, I lost an arrow over there. Go find it for me, he said, and going to look, [Wolf] easily found it and brought it back. Then [Turtle] fixed the arrow as he sat down there, and when he shot it, he hit [the fawn]. And he killed him... As [Wolf] had meant it, he wanted to pay [Turtle], so he asked, Would you like a thigh?... My thigh would hurt and it would kill me, [Turtle] said... Would you like a shoulder? he asked, That, too, my shoulder would hurt and it would kill me, he said... Perhaps the liver, then? he asked, My liver would hurt and it would kill me, he said... The head, then? he asked, My headache would be so bad, it would kill me, he said... [Wolf] got aggravated with him, and said, He doesn't want anything! and without giving him anything, they divided it all and went their separate ways... And then [Turtle] took a small blood clot, wrapped it in leaves, and brought it home. And he had many children and brought it to them. And as he arrived home, they said, Father! Father! as they ran to him... He set it down, and sat down himself... We've gotten a little meat, so cook it for them, he said [to his wife] as he sat... When they went to look, they saw a large package sitting there... Then as they were unwrapping it, nothing was there... Where is it? they asked... Way inside, he said as he sat... They took away all the leaves, and all they found was a small clot of blood... Is this it? they asked... That's what I meant, he said... Goodness, did you think that small amount would be enough for all my sons? she asked, and she slapped the blood in his eyes, and when she did this, he went about saying, My sons, bring me some water... That's why Turtle's eyes turned red, it was said.

29

Girl abducted by Lion

A girl who lives with her brothers is lured by a lion into his boat. When they arrive at his den, he tells her to cook meat in the next house, where she finds an old woman who reveals that she is the meat. Then Lion tells her to fix some acorns. The old woman advises her to put a frog in the pot and to run off. When Lion asks if the acorns are ready, the frog responds. Finally Lion discovers the ruse, and chases after the girl with a stone disk. The youngest brother hears her voice and alerts his older brothers. They all pick up their weapons, but the youngest brother finds only a broken wooden paddle. A woodpecker tells the youngest brother where to hit the disk, and he kills it. They climb a tree and the lion tries to reach them, but as he's climbing up a grapevine, they cut it. They all become the Seven Little Sisters (Pleiades) (cf. Swanton 1929, Creek story 13).

This story is also told among Florida Seminoles, though the sexual aspects of the story are sometimes downplayed. In some versions, it is a boy who is lured away rather than a girl. The story warns about strangers and suggests that even young children can save and be saved if they do exactly as told. As in the first story, it is not age that makes one wise, but discipline and the willingness to listen and observe. Reference to the Pleiades at the end provides a link to the world around us and, as in story 15, explains natural features in terms of human actions.

Este mvnettvlke vnvcomēt vpokvtēs. Mont hoktē hymkusēt omvtēs. Mon mvt mv este mvnettvlken ēwvnwvt omvtēs.

Moman ue-cvokvt hvccet yvyēt omen, mvn uewvn cawet mv hoktē aret omaten... Momof este-papvt ehvs-nērkvn efv echustakucen hayet, mv hvcce uewv mv hoktē cawē araten, hvccet ont omen, mv este-papv tat efv custakuce hayat mv ue-cvokvn perrucen vtehēt 'sak-vlakvtēs.

Momen mv hoktē hēcvtēs. Mont omet em mvlostē tatēs. Momen mv hoktēt okat, Mv efv custakuce cenhecepvranis, kicet omen, Mon omat, perron aohcemket vfvnkuset hēcet omhoyētvnks, kicet omen... Momusen mv hoktē tat mv efucvlken em vlostet okekv, momusen perro iem ohcemkvtēs. Mont mvn okhoyekv, Vfvnkuset hēcet omhoyētvnks, kicen, momusen vfvnkuset hēcet 'sohlikof, perron estos konkon 'sakhepahket, 'svyēpat, mv tis 'sak-vhopvyēcēpen acvmēksvtēs.

Mont Vm vccayvs! [Os]sehpit 'yefulkepvranis, kicvtēs. Mont okat, Hvcce-kenhe hvmken cem vccayarēs! kicet, hvcce aknvrkvpvn 'sak-vyēpvtēs. Mon Vm vccayvs! kicē monkvtēs. Momis, Cem vccayarēs! Vsv vheckan cem vccayarēs! kicet 'svyēpvtēs. Mont 'svyēpet, mv este-papvt ehuten ocepēt omet, mvn likepēt omet vrēpet ohmvtet, mvt este-papv ehute em elecvn ervccayvtēs, mv perro. Momat mvn mv hoktē resorēpvtēs. Mont encukon mv este-papvt resorēpet omekv, mv hoktē ervtvrē eyacekatēs.

Mont omet mv este-papv-vcule tat liket omet okat, mv hoktē mvnette hvte resorēpat okatet, Hompetv hayvs. Vsi cuko likan vpeswv ocēt omēs. Mvn ratahcet noricvs, kicvtēs. Mon mvn okhoyekv, mv hoktē mvnettat

There once lived a group of young men. And there was only one girl. And she was the sister of the young men.

Now the river from which they drew water flowed past, and one day the young girl was getting water there... During this time a lion had made puppies out of his testicles, and he went to the place where the girl drew water, it was a river, and the lion put the puppies he had made in a little boat and came down the river to the place where water was drawn.

And the girl saw him. And she took a liking to [the puppies]. Then the girl said, May I see your little puppies? All right, but you have to climb in the boat and look at them close up, as they usually do, he said... Then because the girl liked the puppies, she climbed into the boat. And again he said, They usually get right up to them and look closely, so as she was looking at them, right up close sitting in the boat, she didn't notice that the boat had been given a shove and had gone quite a distance when she looked up.

Then she said, Dock it for me! I'm getting out and going back. And he said, I'll dock it for you in the next river bend! and they continued down the center of the river. And she kept saying, Dock it for me! But he said, I'll dock it for you! I'll dock it for you over there! he said, and continued on. He continued on, and the lion had a den where he lived, so the lion docked the boat below his den. That's how he brought the young girl there. And as the lion had gotten her to his house, he didn't want her to return home.

Now the old lion sat and said, speaking to the young woman he had taken there, Make something to eat. Over there in that house is meat. Go cut some of it off and cook it, he said. When he told her this, the young

ayvtēs. Eslafkv tat raehset ayvtēs. Ayet mv cuko okhoyat recēyvtēs. Mvn recēyan, hoktạluset liken rem ecēyvtēs. Mohmet mv hoktạlusat em punayvtēs. Momen mv hoktē mvnettat okatet, Mv este-papv-culet okat, Mv cuko ofvn vpeswvt ocēt omēs. Mvn rahopohyet noricvs ca! kicet omen acēyit omis, kicvtēs. Mon mv hoktạlusatet okat, Vnen okēs! Vnen cvpapēt omētok, vnen okhoyēs! kicen... Hēcan mv hoktalat rawarhoyvtē letẹhuset liket oken hēcet takhuervtet raossēpvtēs. Mohmet mv 'ste-papv-culen yem onayvtēs. Yem onayet okat, Sepekan oketskes, kicvtēs. Momen mv momē kicē yem onayan vtēken, Ocēt omētat os tv! mahket ayat, eslafkv ẹ 'mvkaskasēcet aret ayat, mv hoktạluse likē rahēcē eratat mvn okehpvtet mvn rem vkvlafet yesossvtēs. Mohmen mvn ennoricvtēs. Mohmen mvn hompakvtēs.

Mon mv este-papv estvn vrepvranet omet, Lakcvn okcaret takliketskvrēs! kihcet vyēpvtēs. Mont vyēpet omen, mv hoktē mvnettat lakcv okcarvranet arvtēs. Mont omen mv hoktalat okatet em punayvtēs. Mv hoktē mvnettan em punayet okat, Vyepvccvs. Cestemerricvranet omhoyes. Monkv vnen cvpvpẹpet cvlokēpen omat, momusen cēmen cepvpetvn kont omhoyekv, mv lakcv okcarvranetskat omỵlkvn 'tetakuecē poyat, kute-lanucen hopohyet aklihcet, momusen cukon vwvlvpiket vyepetskvrēs, mv hoktalat kicvtēs.

Mon mvn okhoyekv, mv cuko vwvlvpiket vyēpvtēs. Mon sumkēpvten mv este-papv-vcule ervlakvtēs. Mont omis momēn mv hoktē mvnettat sumkepēton kerrekatēs. Momis mvn lakcvn okcarvrēn kihcet ayet omekv, lakcv okcarat akliket omēs komvtēs. Mont omet, Lakcv okcarka? makof, Okcarkepeks! kicet omen, mon okacoks komet mv este-papv-cule tat wakkẹpvtēs. Mont omet, Okcarka? maken, Okcarkeks! kihcen hvtvm

girl went. She got a knife and went. And she went into the house he had meant. And as she entered, she saw a really old lady. Then the old lady spoke with her. And the young girl said, That old lion said, There's meat in that house. Go look for it there and cook it! he said, and that's why I came in here, she said. Then the old lady said, He means me! He eats me, so he means me! she said... As the girl looked, she could see that the old lady had slices cut off of her and looked ragged, so she stood awhile and then came out. Then she returned and told the old lion. She told him, There's nothing out there. As soon as she told him, he said, There is, too! and scraping his knives together, he went to where she had seen the little old lady, and as she had said, he trimmed off pieces of meat and came out. Then she cooked it for him. Then they ate.

The lion was going to go out and said, You stay and fix the acorns! and left. And as he left, the young woman went to fix the acorns. And the old lady spoke to her. She spoke to the young girl, saying, You must go. You will be tormented. Now when he's through eating me, he plans to eat you, so when you've prepared all the acorns that you're fixing, look for a little green frog and put it in [with them], and then go over to the house and leave, the old lady said.

And as she had been told, she went over to the house and left. She was gone when the old lion returned. But he didn't know that the young girl was gone. Because he had left after he had told her to fix the acorns, he thought she was still fixing the acorns. Are the acorns ready? he asked, Not-ready-yet! [the frog] said, and the lion believed the answer and just lay there.* Then, Are the acorns ready? he asked, Not-ready-yet! it said,

* We have translated *okcarkepeks* as 'Not-ready-yet!' to make it sound like a frog. The meaning of this word is uncertain: based on the version recorded by Tuggle (in Swanton 1929:20–21), it might mean 'not leached'.

wakkẹ̄pvtēs. Mont hvtvm, Okcarka? kicen, Okcarkepeks! kicēpen... Kut estometut okcarkeko tayēpet omehaks? mahket, mv este-papv-cule tat momusen cvpvkiket, akhvtapkan kute-lanucet aklikẹ̄pet okehpvtet... Mv este-papv rakhvtapkof, Cēk! mahket kutet aklikẹ̄pet okehpvtet, mv uewvn aaktasiken... Momusen mv este-papv tat cvpakkēt vrēpet omekv, momusen mv uewv tat akhvtvpiket, mv kute aaktaskat akhopoyet akliket, mv kute-lanuce 'sakhēcvtēs.

Mohmet mv kute-lanuce tat aak-ehset cetahket momusen mv hoktē ensumket omat keriyet, vpohet ont omis estomat kerrekatēs. Ẹ̄ mvn vrēpet omvcoks komvyan vtekvtes kihocen aret, momusen motvkvn licepēt omatet, momusen eraehset nene vpeyạkusat erohhuericat, tvr-takuset erlvtkẹ̄pen 'saret nene vpeyakat vtēkat respohyet... Momusen cuko-homvn rasatet resvlahket cukon vwvlvpecihcen, Mvtaten 'svyẹ̄pvtēs. Mohmen mvn 'sayet omen, momusen mv este-papv-cule tat momusen mvn yopv huyiret vcak-ayet okat,

> Motvkv cakka,
> Motvkv cakka!

maket yopv tat este-papv-cule tat werwēyẹ̄pvtēs. Mon mv nake motvkv tat momusen mv hoktē estensumkatet cakkepvranet omen... Mv hoktē tat ayusē hayet ont omis, cakkepvranē tvlket omēpen, mv hoktē yvhikvtēs. Mont oket,

> Pvne ostē lecv cvcertake vpokē orvko,
> Calekv,
> Calekv,

and kept lying there. Now again, Are they ready? he asked, Not-ready-yet! it said... Why is it not ready? he asked, and the lion, now angry, went down [to the water] and found it had been a little green frog sitting there talking... When the lion went down [to see], he heard a Cheek! and saw it had been the frog sitting down there, and it jumped into the water... Then the lion was going about really furious, so he got in the water and looked where the frog had jumped in, and found the frog.

Then he took the frog out of the water and mashed it, and he knew that he had lost the young girl, and though he asked, he didn't find out what happened. I'm sure she is out there somewhere, he said, and having a motaka [stone disk], he took it and when he stood it up on a little trail, it just made a rattling sound and fell and he tried all the trails...* Then he brought it back to the front of the house and made it go over the house, and then it finally took off. So as it went, the old lion followed right behind singing,

> Motaka catch up,
> Motaka catch up!

and flopped along behind it. Now that motaka was about to catch up with the girl who had gone away... The girl tried to keep going, but she knew that it was overtaking her and she began to sing. She sang,

> I won't reach the four ravines where my brothers live below,
> For I die,
> For I die,

---

* *Motaka* (Creek *motvkv*) is an old word referring to a chunky stone (Haas ca. 1940) used in a game. It is used in a similar way to find someone in a Natchez story (Swanton 1929:226).

maket yvhikvtēs. Momis mv ecertake 'svcolvkuecat pohvkekon, mv mvnettvlke ecuse mahhet cu̧tkusēt arēt omvtēs. Momen mvt ahkopanat mvt fettvn arvtēs. Moman mvt pohvtēs. Mont okatet, Powvnwv pun-sumkvnna omēn yvhikes, maket mv ervhvlken em onayvtēs. Mon okaket, Mahkēskos cē. Estomhoyvtē estofvt omēs, kicaken raossvtēs.

Mont fettvn ahkopanet aret onkv, hvtvm aret oman, mvn yvhikan pohet okēpan okhoyekv... Hvtvm maken okvyan okatskekv hvtvm yvhiket os. Monkv mapohicvkēs, maket vnvcomvtēken 'seste-naoricet omen... Eston okehaks? kohmet, mapohicakan makēpen okehpvten mapohicakan mvt okēpvnto omēt on okēpen hęren mapohicakan,

    Pvne ostē lecv cvcertake vpokē orvkot,
    Cvcertake vpokē orvko,
    Calekv,
    Calekv,

makępuset yvhikępet okēpen... Momusen, Naket em estomen arē hęret okēpvntut os, mahket... Moman 'yvwolicepēt yvhikępet oken pohakat, momusen nake esnvfkvkē tayat nak pocuswv omis cawet pefathoken, momusen nake esnafkē nake 'sēyvnicvkē tayat 'setetayehpet vpeyephoyen... Momusen mv estuce cępanusat Naken omvranvya? maket lētket aret omis, naket enheckekon aret hompetv-hak-cukon erecēyan, mvn vtapv kvlkusēt vsokkvten mvn 'rem vtasiket eraesehpet lētkvtēs. Mont vpeyephoyaten yopvn alētkat, mvo ervnrapet fulhoyen erorvtēs.

Momof mv nake motvkv kihocat aassēcēpat mvo vlvkēpen, Nafket monkat estomēcet komat momēcakēto estomis, estomēcvkeko tayen vrēpen... Mv cēpvnusat lētket rorof, fuswvt tuskucē hocefkēt tvmket ho-yanet omat... Toktus hel, hel! Toktus hel, hel! maket eshoyahnet 'sayet

she sang. Though her oldest brothers did not hear, there was a younger brother. Now he was outside playing. And he heard her. And he told his brothers, Our long-lost sister is singing. And they said, Don't say that. Whatever happened to her is forever, they told him, and he came back out.

And he continued to play outside, and again he heard her singing for sure... I said I heard her, and you didn't think it was her, and now she's singing again. So listen, he said, bothering the brothers several times... What is he talking about? they wondered, and they listened and heard what he had heard, they listened carefully and heard her sing as she used to sing,

    I won't reach the four valleys where my brothers live below,
    Where my brothers live,
    For I die,
    For I die,

she kept singing... Then they said, Something's really gone wrong for her. Now when they could hear her singing close by, they ran and gathered all kinds of clubs and axes, and each had something to hit it [the motaka] with... Then the little boy ran around asking, What am I going to use? but couldn't find anything and went into the kitchen where he found a wooden paddle with a part missing that was wedged into something up high, and he jumped to reach it. As they had already gone, he ran after them, and finally caught up with the others as they were meeting it.

Then as the thing called motaka that had chased after her was getting there, they hit it and did everything they knew to do, and yet couldn't stop it... Then as the little boy came running up, a small speckled woodpecker flew by... Toktus heel, heel! Toktus heel, heel! it said as it went omen okat, mv cēpanat oket, Ele-toktuswvn ennafkvkan ēlusvnts, maket oks ca! mahket, mv vtapv-kvlkuce ēsvtēt mv nake aran ele-toktuswvn 'sennafkat est-akhēckv omēt aret ohmvten... Mvn ele-toktuswvn 'sennafkat, momusen svmahlusen vpoyvtēs.

Momehcet ohmen fullet eto hueren vcemēcet oh-vpoken, este-papv-vcule tat vlahket aret mv eto cemecē oh-vpokan, mv elecvn vlaket omet, Iecencemkepvranvkis, kicen, Mv pvrko-fvkvn vcemket omvkis, kicaken, aret vcemken entahcet aswihket, momusen hvlwēcvtēt omēs. Mon kolas-cuklofkv haket omvtēstvnts, mahokvnts cē. Monkv estet omistvnts, mahokvnts cē.

past,* and the boy said, He says if you hit him in the heel he'll die! and he took the broken paddle he had grabbed and hit the thing on the heel and they found that it had been like a mirror... As he hit its heel with the paddle, the thing shattered in a heap.

After this they climbed up in a tree and were sitting there, and the old lion came to where they sat in the tree they had climbed and coming below them, said, I want to climb up there with you. We climbed up on that grapevine, they said, and as he climbed up, they cut the vine and made him fall, and immediately they went high into [the sky]. And they became the Seven Little Sisters, it was said. So they were people, it was said.

---

* When the woodpecker says *Toktus hel, hel!* in Creek, it sounds like *ele-toktuswv* 'its ankle', so the boy knows to aim for the ankle. To make the woodpecker's hint work in English, we have changed it to *Toktus heel, heel!* and had the boy aim for the heel.

References

Aarne, Antti, and Stith Thompson. 1964. *The Types of the Folktale: A Classification and Bibliography*. 2d rev. ed. Folklore Fellows Communications, no. 184. Helsinki: Academia Scientarum Fennica.

Baker, T. Lindsay, and Julie P. Baker, eds. 1996. *The WPA Oklahoma Slave Narratives*. Norman: University of Oklahoma Press.

Bascom, William. 1992. *African Folktales in the New World*. Bloomington and Indianapolis: Indiana University Press.

Buckner, H. F. 1860. *A Grammar of the Maskωke, or Creek Language, to Which are Prefixed Lessons in Spelling, Reading, and Defining*. Marion, Ala.: Domestic and Indian Mission Board.

Clark, Carter Blue. 1979. "Opothleyahola and the Creeks during the Civil War." In *Indian Leaders: Oklahoma's First Statesmen*. Edited by H. Glenn Jordan and Thomas M. Holm, 49–63. Oklahoma City: Oklahoma Historical Society.

Debo, Angie. 1941. *The Road to Disappearance: A History of the Creek Indians*. The Civilization of the American Indian Series. Norman: University of Oklahoma Press.

Dundes, Alan. 1969. "African Tales among the North American Indians." *Southern Folklore Quarterly* 29:207–19.

Grantham, Bill. 2002. *Creation Myths and Legends of the Creek Indians*. Gainesville: University Press of Florida.

Haas, Mary R. 1939. Creek Field Notes. Vol. 15. Papers of Mary R. Haas. American Philosophical Society Library, Philadelphia, Ms Coll 094.

————. ca. 1940. Creek Vocabulary. American Philosophical Society Library, Philadelphia, Ms Coll 094.

Hodge, F. W. 1923. Report of the Ethnologist-in-Charge. *Thirty-seventh Annual Report, Bureau of American Ethnology, 1915–16*. Washington, D.C.

Jumper, Betty Mae. 1994. *Legends of the Seminoles*. Sarasota, Fla.: Pineapple Press.

Kroeber, Karl. 1981. "An Introduction to the Art of Traditional American Indian Narration." In *Traditional Literatures of the American Indian: Texts and Interpretations*. Edited and compiled by Karl Kroeber, pp. 1–24. Lincoln: University of Nebraska Press.

Lankford, George E. 1987. *Native American Legends. Southeastern Legends: Tales from the Natchez, Caddo, Biloxi, Chickasaw, and Other Nations*. The American Folklore Series, W. K. McNeil, Gen. Ed. Little Rock: August House.

Lewis, David, Jr., and Ann Jordan. 2002. *Creek Indian Medicine Ways: The Enduring Power of Mvskoke Religion*. Albuquerque: University of New Mexico Press.

Martin, Howard N. 1977. *Myths and Folktales of the Alabama-Coushatta Indians of Texas*. Austin: Encino Press.

Martin, Jack B. 1997. Interview with Felix Gouge, January 22.

Martin, Jack B., and Margaret McKane Mauldin. 2000. *A Dictionary of Creek/ Muskogee, with Notes on the Florida and Oklahoma Seminole Dialects of Creek*. Studies in the Anthropology of North American Indians, R. J. DeMallie and Douglas R. Parks, eds. Lincoln: University of Nebraska Press.

Meserve, John Bartlett. 1931. "Chief Opothleyahola." Chronicles of Oklahoma 9:439–53.

Mooney, James. 1900. *Myths of the Cherokee*. Nineteenth Annual Report. Bureau of American Ethnology, 1897–98. Washington, D.C.

Robertson, William Schenck, and David Winslett. 1867. *Nakcokv Es Kerretv Enhvteceskv. Muskokee or Creek First Reader*. 2d ed. New York: Mission House. Reprinted: Okmulgee, Okla.: B. Frank Belvin, Baptist Home Mission Board, 1963.

———. 1871. *Mvskoke Nakcokv Eskerretv Esvhokkolat. Creek Second Reader*. New York: American Tract Society. Reprinted: Okmulgee, Okla.: B. Frank Belvin, Baptist Home Mission Board, 1972.

Speck, Frank G. 1907. *The Creek Indians of Taskigi Town*. Memoirs of the American Anthropological Association 2, no. 8, part 2. Lancaster, Pa.: American Anthropological Association. Reprinted: Millwood, N.Y.: Kraus Reprint Co., 1974.

Swanton, John R. 1922. *Early History of the Creek Indians and Their Neighbors*. Bureau of American Ethnology Bulletin No. 73. Washington, D.C.

———. 1928. *Religious Beliefs and Medicinal Practices of the Creek Indians*. Forty-second Annual Report, Bureau of American Ethnology, 1924–25. Washington, D.C.

———. 1929. *Myths and Tales of the Southeastern Indians*. Washington, D.C.: Smithsonian Bureau of American Ethnology. Reprinted: Norman and London: University of Oklahoma Press, 1995.

Thompson, Stith. 1955–58. *The Motif-index of Folk-literature; A Classification of Narrative Elements in Folktales, Ballads, Myths, Fables, Mediaeval Romances, Exempla, Fabliaux, Jest-books, and Local Legends*. Rev. and enl. ed. 6 vols. Bloomington: Indiana University Press.

Tuggle, W. O. 1973. *Shem, Ham & Japheth: The Papers of W. O. Tuggle*. Edited by Eugene Current-Garcia. Athens, Ga.: University of Georgia Press.

Wagner, Günter. 1931. *Yuchi Tales*. Publications of the American Ethnological Society, 13. New York: G. E. Stechert.